PICTORIAL HISTORY
OF WORLD WAR II

*The graphic record of your Armed
Forces in action throughout every
phase of the global conflict*

Volume I

The War in Europe

1952

ACKNOWLEDGEMENTS

All photographs are official Department of Defense, U.S. Coast
Guard, U.S. Air Force, U.S. Army, U.S. Marine Corps or U.S.
Navy except as follows:

ACME NEWSPICTURES, INC.: 5, 58, 120, 121, 135, 165, 208, 209, 220, 221, 236, 245.

BRITISH COMBINE PHOTOS, LTD.: 35, 46, 144, 145.

INTERNATIONAL NEWS PHOTOS: 21 (lower), 344, 345.

NEW YORK "NEWS'" 367.

ODHAMS PRESS: 6, 8, 10, 11, 12, 13, 14, 15, 16, 17, 18, 19, 20, 21 (upper), 22, 23, 24, 25, 26, 27, 28, 29, 30, 31, 32, 33, 34, 36, 37, 38, 39, 40, 41, 42, 43, 44, 45, 47, 48, 49, 50, 51, 52, 53, 54, 55, 56, 57, 61, 62, 63, 64, 65, 66, 67, 68, 69, 70, 71, 72, 73, 74, 75, 76, 77, 78, 79, 80, 81, 82, 83, 84, 85, 87, 88, 89, 90, 91, 92, 95, 96, 97, 98, 99, 100, 101, 102, 103, 105, 106, 107, 108, 110, 111, 112, 113, 114, 115, 116, 117, 118, 119, 122, 123, 124, 125, 126, 127, 128, 129, 130, 131, 132, 133, 134, 136, 137, 138, 139, 140, 141, 142, 143, 146, 147, 148, 149, 154, 155, 162, 163, 166, 167, 168, 169, 171, 172, 173, 174, 175, 178, 179, 180, 181, 188, 189, 195, 196, 197, 212, 213, 218, 219, 222, 223, 226, 230, 231, 304, 372, 373.

PRESS ASSOCIATION, INC.: 7 (upper), 9 (upper), 104, 331, 364, 380, 384.

SOVFOTO: 150, 151.

WIDE WORLD PHOTOS, INC.: 7 (lower).

WE ARE GRATEFUL!

To the 15,000,000 gallant men and women of the Armed Forces who served heroically in the defense of their country over land, sea, and in the air from the dismal day at Pearl Harbor to the final, unconditional surrender of the Axis Powers in 1945.

These volumes are humbly dedicated.

CONTENTS

COLOR PLATES

YOUR GROUND FORCES IN ACTION

By General of the Army George C. Marshall

DURING World War II the United States assembled, trained, and deployed into action the greatest fighting force in history. One of the most important elements of this juggernaut which brought victory after carrying the war across two oceans and into the heart of the enemies' territory was our Army Ground Forces.

In both words and pictures this volume tells something of the story of the foot soldier—of these brave men who fought so close to the enemy that they came to know the very color of his eyes. Words and pictures, are, of course, inadequate to portray their valor, but they do offer tangible evidence of the fighting skill and heroism of which America is proud.

Like his comrades in our fighting Navy, Marine Corps, Army Air Arm, and other services contributing to victory, the American ground soldier was rushed to a maturity for which he had not planned or even dreamed. He had been a student, a mechanic, an accountant, a farmer, and he was transformed suddenly into a soldier. His native resourcefulness and competitive spirit were so great that he conquered—on the ground, face to face and weapon to weapon—those enemy veterans whose military training and entire upbringing had been planned and unhurriedly developed to one end.

The world knows how well he did the job. He needed not only the personal courage for hand to hand fighting, but a high degree of skill to make him proficient in the use of complicated mechanisms to fit himself into the ground-tank-air-sea team. He took the ground and held it. He conquered, and imposed his will on the conquered. He shed most of the war's sweat and blood—his family shed the tears.

In August, 1940, Japan's army approximated 120 divisions. It was busily entrenching itself on the Asiatic mainland, and openly fortifying its outlying Pacific islands, most of which we later took at a heavy price.

On the other side of the world a jubilant Nazi army of about 300 divisions was enjoying a brief rest before its planned attack on Britain across the English Channel. In one short year this army had crushed Poland, Denmark, Norway, Holland, and Belgium, and had disposed of France in six weeks. Italy, with about 70 divisions, had just declared war, and was readying to strike the British in Egypt. To many, the axis military machine appeared invincible. In Western Europe, England alone remained free, and many doubted that she could stave off defeat.

At that time the ground fighting forces of the United States consisted of 28 poorly-equipped divisions (10 Regular and 18 National Guard) scattered in small units throughout the country and on isolated overseas bases. Our Air Force consisted of some partially-equipped squadrons serving continental United States, Panama, Hawaii, and the Philippines; their planes were largely obsolescent and probably could not have survived a day of modern aerial combat. In short, though the world was rife with aggression and force, we were less than a third-rate military power.

And yet, three years later our forces grew to carry the fight to the enemy all around the world, and forced him to the unconditional surrender to which this nation and its Allies had dedicated themselves. During the last two years of the war the victorious advance of the United States sea, air and land forces, together with those of our Allies, was virtually unchecked. They controlled the skies and the seas and no army could successfully oppose them. Behind these forces was the output of American farms and factories, exceeding any similar effort of man, so that the peoples everywhere with whom we were joined in the fight for decency and justice were able to reinforce their efforts through the aid of American ships, food, munitions and supplies.

Whether, because of these successes, this generation of Americans will keep in mind the black days of 1942 when the Japanese conquered all of Malaysia, occupied Burma and threatened India, while the German armies approached the Volga and the Suez, is open to question. Yet in those hours Germany and Japan came so close to complete domination of the world that we do not yet realize how thin the thread of Allied survival was stretched.

Though our effort was stupendous after Pearl Harbor—indeed, though it finally swung the scales to victory for the Allies—we can in good conscience take little credit for our part in staving off disaster in those early, critical days. It is certain that the refusal of our Allies to accept what appeared to be inevitable defeat was the great factor in the salvage of our own civilization. The security of the United States of America was saved by vast oceans, by Allies, and by the errors of the enemy. For probably the last time in the history of the world those ocean distances were a vital factor in our defense. If we elect again to depend on others and the whim and error of potential enemies, we will be carrying the treasure and freedom of this great nation in a fragile bag.

It was during those dark days that the American citizen who was to play so important a role as a ground soldier was forged into the fighting man who is respected and feared throughout the world. The magnitude of the task of hastily transforming citizens into sodliers is almost beyond comprehension. Faced on nearly every hand with highly trained and veteran enemies, the American high command hastily explored every means of raising, training and equipping forces that would carry the war to our enemies.

To do this job better and quicker, a reorganization was effected, out of which came the Army Ground Forces, as such, on March 9, 1942. Under one head this combined the Infantry, Field Artillery, Cavalry, Tank Destroyers, Coast Artillery (including Antiaircraft Artillery), and Armored Force. So organized, the Ground Forces grew to a strength of 89 divisions with a veritable host of auxiliary fighting and administrative units. These, for whom the fighting never ceased, absorbed 81 percent of the Army's battle losses. The infantry, which comprised only 20.5 percent of the total strength overseas, suffered 70 percent of the total casualties. These ground soldiers made more than 40 major amphibious landings on hostile shores, and captured and disarmed more than 8,000,000 enemy troops. Though many of them had never previously been in battle, their period of training in the United States had been so realistic that, finally face to face with the enemy, they acquitted themselves like veterans. Patton's famous sweep across France was largely carried out by troops who never before had been engaged in battle.

World War II was the most technological of all man's struggles, but it put just as much emphasis on the ground soldier as did those wars waged with the short sword and the musket. It proved conclusively, I think, that as long as men walk on the earth, use wheeled transportation, or must return to the earth to maintain themselves, it is fundamental that land warfare and the soldier with his feet on the ground will have a high priority in the conduct of war. Certainly, if within the foreseeable future this country should again be forced into combat, the ground soldier will then, as before, mark our progress along the path to victory.

YOUR AIR FORCE IN ACTION

By General of the Army H. H. Arnold

MODERN warfare on a global scale involves not only Ground, Naval, and Air Forces but civilians of all walks of life. The danger zone of modern war is not restricted to battle lines and adjacent areas but extends to the innermost parts of a nation.

The development of air power has greatly lessened the value of natural barriers and static defense installations, for aircraft can deliver devastating blows at centers of population, industry, and government. The initial attack of Germany on Poland, 1 September 1939, and the Japanese attack on Pearl Harbor, 7 December 1941, that drew the United States into World War II were both aerial attacks. It is significant that the last important action of the war, the dropping of the atomic bombs on Hiroshima and Nagasaki, was also an air operation.

While it would not be true to say that World War II was won entirely by air power, it is true that American air power, supported by American industry and the American people, made a unique and positive contribution to victory. Air power shortened the war and was responsible for an enormous saving in American lives and in the material of warfare.

When the Japanese made their surprise attack on Pearl Harbor, the United States was not as a nation prepared for war. But defeat there, was a signal for unprecedented effort. The Army Air Forces, instrument of American air power, was developed into a destructive force unparalleled in history by hundred-fold expansion and development in the comparatively brief space of four years. Time was on our side—because our allies held the enemy in Europe until we were prepared to engage him. Space was on our side—because in 1941 the natural barrier of distance had not been overcome by our enemies as it has since been overcome by us, with our aircraft capable of flying 10,000 miles. Today Japanese and German cities lie in ruins, monuments to the destructiveness of air power and reminders that without adequate air power to protect them our own cities could become ruins in a future war.

LESSONS OF WORLD WAR II

FROM the experience of World War II certain lessons are to be learned. Most important is the lesson that the only defense against attack by

air power is superior air power. The peacetime mission of the Air Force is to achieve superiority for American air power and thereby to contribute to the security of the United States. Certain requirements essential to the success of that mission should become more generally appreciated.

Air power is not composed alone of the war-making components of aviation. It is the total aviation activity of a nation — civilian and military, commercial and private, potential as well as existing. It includes a nation's ability to deliver cargo, people, destructive missiles, and war-making potential through the air to a desired destination to accomplish a desired purpose.

Military air power—or air force—is dependent upon the air potential provided by industry which, in turn, thrives best in an atmosphere of individual initiative and free enterprise. The remarkable development of American air power during World War II is a tribute to American industry and to American labor. At the present time plans for the defense of America include the prime requirement of industrial preparedness. Particularly would a vast expansion of the aviation industry in a time of war be a major necessity under present conditions of warfare.

An air force is also dependent upon science, upon scientific research and the application of its results, to advance theory, technical knowledge, and the material of aerial warfare. The rate of obsolescence of air force materiel is exceptionally rapid. Today as another essential of national defense we have an intensive program of scientific research and development.

A modern air force must have flexibility of basic structure, which will permit it to adapt itself successfully to the changes which are certain to come in the foreseeable future. Whatever its numerical size—and today it is negligible in comparison to what it was on V-E day, 1945—our Air Force must be second to none in range and striking power or in the efficiency of its organization. Experiences of World War II have suggested the basic organization of the peacetime Air Force which was effected within five months after the end of the war.

Above all, air leaders must have a clear understanding of the strategic concept of air power. The theory upon which we based our major air operations in World War II and on which are based all plans for our present and future defense was not new when first employed in the war. Its application, however, was new; and in the course of the war the original concept was greatly extended. Our strategic bombing attacks on our enemies so depleted their specific industrial and economic resources and so weakened the will of their people to resist that continued resistance became useless, perhaps impossible. Particularly as employed against Japan was the concept proved by the results. Japan surrendered unconditionally with large armies undefeated and in control of nearly three million square miles of land populated by 500,000,000 people. The war was won without the necessity for an invasion.

EMPLOYMENT OF STRATEGIC CONCEPT

IN THE following pages men who were leaders in the winning of World War II tell in part how the strategic concept was employed to gain air superiority and how strategic attack and tactical operations were thereafter applied to the defeat of the enemy. Text and pictures will revive for readers memories of four bitter years we cannot afford to forget. If we remember them well enough, we shall determine with firmer resolve to maintain air power adequate to forbid aggression and to guard the peace that is priceless to the peoples of all the world.

A DICTATOR SPEAKS. The first stirrings of the Nazi plot to conquer the world gained much of its momentum from the personal magnetism of Adolf Hitler, the greatest tyrant of modern times. In this picture taken (in 1936) at a Nurnberg congress, der Fuehrer, using a somewhat forceful gesture, is shown addressing adherents in the Luitpold Arena, with the Nazi swastika outlined boldly on the platform.

TENSION . . . THEN WAR. Anxious faces line pavement as Neville Chamberlain, in the Cabinet Room of Number 10 Downing Street, began the announcement of Britain's declaration of war. Almost as he finished speaking, the wail of air raid sirens all over the country electrified an already tense atmosphere. It was a false alarm, and soon the sirens sounded the "all clear" signal. No declaration of war could have been more dramatic.

LOOKING WAR IN THE FACE. Unready but unafraid, the British accept the war that, by their treaties, was automatically thrust upon them when Hitler's armies invaded Poland. UPPER. The War Proclamation being read from the steps of the Royal Exchange while crowds listen solemnly. LOWER. Bewildered groups of persons in front of Number Ten Downing Street shortly after the Prime Minister's announcement that England was at war with Germany.

WHERE GERMAN U-BOAT STRUCK. Hours after the declaration of war, a German U-Boat claimed its first victim. With no warning, the liner "Athenia" bound for Montreal from Belfast with more than 1,000 passengers, was sunk. German propaganda put out the story that a British sub, on Winston Churchill's order, had committed the deed to influence American public opinion. About 112 persons were lost. The rest were rescued by ships hurrying to her assistance. The "Athenia" is seen settling down by the stern.

SIXIEME ÉDITION

L'INTRANSIGEANT

6ᵉ édition

le Journal de Paris

50

50

LA GUERRE

DEPUIS CE MATIN 11 HEURES

L'ANGLETERRE est en état de guerre avec L'ALLEMAGNE

omme il avait été prévu, après la dernière démarche de ambassadeur britannique à Berlin, notre représentant a dressé au Reich la même et ultime injonction dont
LE DELAI EXPIRE A 17 HEURES

WAR'S HEADLINES SCREAM IN FRANCE. The front pages of newspapers around the globe announced the news that England had already been at war since 11 A.M. and that France's ultimatum would expire at 5 o'clock that afternoon. But such events as the sinking of the "Athenia" by a German U-Boat had set the wheels of preparation turning the world over. The Atlantic Ocean disaster cost 112 lives, 30 of which were Americans. Public sentiment in the United States was greatly aroused by the incident. UPPER. The French newspaper "L'Intransigeant" headlines the news of that day on its front page. LOWER. A boatload of survivors from the ill-fated "Athenia" being brought to Ireland on a rescue tender.

HORSE-DRAWN ARTILLERY ADVANCES. To economize on gasoline the Germans used thousands of horse-drawn carts to follow their mechanized units during the Polish campaign. In the picture above, the Germans seem to be finding the Polish road, churned up by their own tanks and armored cars, difficult to travel. Here a German gun team is depicted crossing a Polish river over a bridge left intact by retreating Poles.

POLISH INFANTRY ATTACKING. In spite of their great fighting qualities and powers of endurance, the embattled Polish Army could do little to check the enemy's armored columns. Nevertheless, they courageously faced a tremendously superior enemy in an heroic and hopeless attempt to defend their homeland. The picture (above) depicts the Polish infantry charging resolutely forward to the attack.

POLISH FORTRESS YIELDS TO GERMAN SALVOS. For six days and six nights the 11-inch guns of the German battleship "Schleswig-Holstein" bombarded the Polish fort of Westerplatte, on the outskirts of Danzig, at point-blank range (right), while from the land and air furious assaults were made by large and well-equipped German forces. For six days the Poles held out, but on the morning of the seventh, the commander of the garrison surrendered to save what was left of his men. It was estimated that the German land forces alone amounted to a division, whereas the defenders, all told, numbered only a company. The picture above shows the Nazi flag being hoisted by German soldiers over the shell-torn battlements after the garrison surrendered. Danzig had fallen only two weeks before the Polish fort and munitions dump yielded to the German Wehrmacht. Soon after the United States, determined though she was to avoid war, began preparing for any eventuality. On September 8, the President declared a limited national emergency, and authorized the recall of officers, men and nurses in the reserve to active duty.

B.E.F. LANDS IN FRANCE. The plans for the transportation of men and materiel to France had been drawn up by the French and British General Staffs long before the war clouds broke, so that when war was declared it only remained to put them into operation. With great speed—and even greater secrecy—men, guns, tanks, and all the equipment needed to maintain an army in the field, were shipped across the Channel. It was not until September 12, by which time most of the materiel had arrived, that the British people learned of the secret. This picture depicts troops and guns being disembarked at a French port. Viscount Gort, V.C., was appointed Commander-in-Chief of the British armies in France, under the supreme command of General Maurice Gustave Gamelin. Lord Gort was made Commander-in-Chief of the British Expeditionary Force immediately after the war started. He had the distinction of having won more medals on the field than any other British officer covering a period of 40 years. General Gamelin was Commander-in-Chief of the Allied Armies, and former chief of the French national defense, before assuming supreme command in France.

THE "COURAGEOUS" GOES DOWN. H.M. Aircraft Carrier "Courageous" was struck amidships by a torpedo from a German submarine while on patrol duty on September 17, and sank within a short time. Orders to abandon ship were given five minutes after she was struck, but her Commander, Captain Mackeig-Jones, remained on the bridge and tra-

ditionally went down with his ship. The picture (above) shows
the "Courageous" heeling over shortly before her death
plunge; her crew can be clearly seen scrambling down the side
into the water. The "Courageous" had a full complement consisting on 1,126 officers and men; 515 lost their lives in the
British Royal Navy's first major loss of World War II.

BOMBED POLISH ARMORED TRAIN. This remarkable picture shows graphically the destruction to a Polish armored train after an attack by a Nazi bomber. High explosive bombs were used. Their effect can be seen by the train damage and size of the crater.

GERMANS IN MOP-UP OPERATION. Though the Poles were hopelessly outmanned, it took Hitler's troops a month before they could force the Polish capital to surrender. A primary reason for the success of the Germans was close co-operation between masses of mechanized forces and hundreds of bombing planes. Despite severe deficiencies in both these arms, the Poles resisted valiantly. UPPER. German artillerymen batter their way through the outskirts of the city. LOWER. Infantry advance on a Warsaw street under cover of tanks.

WARSAW'S RESISTANCE ENDS. Though the Germans claimed to have surrounded Warsaw by September 15, it was not until the 27th that the capital, battered by aerial and artillery bombardment, was forced to capitulate. On that day, high Polish and German officials of both armies met in a bus on the outskirts of the city and arranged terms of surrender.

Three days later the remnants of the heroic Polish garrison marched out of the city, then occupied by Nazi troops. The picture shows the disarmed soldiers marching dejectedly out of the capital they had so bravely defended, as equally dejected civilians stand by. Division of Poland came shortly after surrender.

A NEW DIVISION OF POLAND. Poland was again divided among her neighbors when, on September 29, German Foreign Minister Joachim von Ribbentrop in Moscow signed a second Soviet - German agreement defining the boundaries of the German and Soviet occupied areas of the country. The map (right) shows how the territory was divided. UPPER. V. M. Molotov, then Russian Premier, signs the agreement on behalf of the Soviets. Behind him stand Ribbentrop and Marshal Stalin. Germany took not only Danzig and the Polish Corridor, but Warsaw and vast areas to the south which had never had any German population. Russia claimed the area east of Brest-Litovsk, an area predominantly Ukrainian, and almost identical with that bounded by the famous "Curzon Line." This line had been suggested as the frontier between Poland and Russia by Lord Curzon in 1920. Germany obtained all the coal mines and industrial areas, while Russia obtained the Galicia oil fields. This was the fourth partition of Poland in her history. Poland had cost the Germans over 91,000 killed, and 98,000 wounded. The German air force lost 1,000 planes, while the armored troops lost approximately 1,400 tanks. Polish losses in missing, wounded, and killed numbered 181,000. Ten months later, after Germany had attacked Russia, the Soviets declared the treaty of partition abrogated.

NAZI CONQUERORS IN SILENT WARSAW. On October 5, Hitler flew to Warsaw to take the salute at the Grand Review of his victorious troops. The route was carefully chosen to avoid those parts of the city that had been devastated by aerial bombardment. The streets were lined by Nazi troops to keep expected crowds in check. It was an unnecessary precaution since Warsaw's population stayed indoors, and the procession made its way through almost deserted streets.

UNDERSEA RAIDERS HONORED. A reception honoring Lieutenant Prien, commander of the U-Boat which torpedoed H.M.S. "Royal Oak," and his crew is staged by Berliners. By a feat of daring to which Winston Churchill himself paid tribute, the German submarine penetrated the defenses of Scapa Flow and torpedoed the ship October 14. "It appears probable," said Mr. Churchill, speaking to the House of Commons, as First Lord of the Admiralty, "that the U-Boat fired three or four torpedoes of which only one hit the bow. Twenty minutes later the U-Boat fired three or four additional torpedoes, and these, striking in quick succession, caused the ship to capsize and sink." Eight hundred and ten British seamen lost their lives in the sinking.

FRENCH AND GERMAN PATROLS AT WORK. Although during the first few months of the war there were no large scale actions on the Western Front, patrols from both sides were constantly seeking information concerning the strength and disposition of the opposing forces. In both pictures patrols are seen moving through a village on reconnaissance.

ATTEMPT ON LIFE OF HITLER. On November 8, Hitler unexpectedly decided to attend a meeting held in the Buergerbraukeller, a beer hall in Munich, to celebrate the anniversary of the Nazi "putsch" of 1923. After making a violently anti-British speech, he left the building at 9:15 P.M. with high ranking Nazi party members. Twenty minutes later a bomb, which had been concealed in one of the supporting pillars, shattered the building, causing the ceiling to collapse on the assembly. Many attending the meeting were Hitler's earliest

supporters. Nine persons were killed, and more than sixty injured. The German authorities accused the British Secret Service of responsibility for the plot; large rewards were offered for information leading to the arrest of the conspirators. The workmen who had prepared the hall for the meeting and others were arrested. Whether this was a genuine attempt on the Fuehrer's life or just another "stunt" to increase his popularity, we will never know. At the left Hitler is seen speaking. The picture above gives some idea of the effect of the bomb.

SCRATCH ONE U-BOAT. Despite all Germany's efforts to step up her submarine warfare, she was never able to enjoy successes in undersea technique comparable to those of the first World War. Because of new methods of detection, the British Royal Navy continued to succeed in anti-submarine warfare. During the early months of the war Germany lost an average of three submarines a week. These photographs show a U-Boat surfaced, and boats picking up the survivors.

RUSSIAN INVASION OF FINLAND. On November 30,
lightning struck Finland. Russian bombers darkened the sky
over Helsinki and began wholesale destruction of a large
part of the nation. One of the war's first tragedies, Finland
fought Russia, against great odds, then, later, plunged into
another ordeal of destruction by entering the world conflict
as an ally of Germany. ABOVE. A block of flats in Helsinki
blazes furiously after being hit by a high explosive bomb.

GUTTED HULK OF "GRAF SPEE." By international law, a belligerent warship in time of war may not stay in a neutral port for more than a specified time, and the whole world waited expectantly for the "Graf Spee" to come out of Montevideo harbor to join in a naval encounter with the British cruisers "Exeter," "Ajax," and "Achilles." The British ships lay in wait outside anxious to engage the German vessel and finish the job they had begun so well. But it was not to be. On the evening of December 17, the "Graf Spee" steamed out of the harbor, but not, as was expected, to seaward where the British ships lay in wait, but towards the west. Shortly after 8 P.M. two explosions shook the air and a flame shot skyward. The ship was blotted from view by a dense cloud of black smoke as she crumpled up, a mass of twisted steel. She had been scuttled by her commander on express orders from

Hitler. Such was the inglorious end of one of the proudest ships of the German Navy. For his brilliant conduct of the battle Commodore Sir Henry Harwood received the Order of the Bath and was promoted to Rear Admiral. Captain Hans Langsdorff, Commander of the "Graf Spee," could not endure his shame. Two days after he had given the order to scuttle his ship, he committed suicide. In scuttling the ship, Captain Langsdorff had transferred his crew to barges, and pressed an electric contact which exploded the "Spee." Sixty-two British prisoners aboard the "Spee" were set free and Great Britain rejoiced over the naval victory. The German crew were all arrested and taken into custody by the Uruguayan government. The picture (above) shows the blazing wreck of the pocket battleship hours after the explosion in Montevideo's harbor.

FINNISH SKI-TROOPS AT THE FRONT. The skill and audacity shown by Finnish ski detachments was one of the outstanding tactical maneuvers of the Russo-Finnish War. Each man was a skilled sportsman as well as soldier. Their agility over snow-glutted terrain enabled them to penetrate enemy lines. The fearful cold in which they fought is attested by the Russian corpses (lower).

FROM NORTH OF THE BORDER. The first of many Canadian Air Force units assigned to England arrived during the last two weeks of December. Their purpose was to prepare camps and training fields for new Canadian air arms. By 1939, 7,000 recruits, Canadian and American, had applied for duty with the R.C.A.F. Acknowledging British cheerios, the airmen in the picture (above) wave back good naturedly as they step ashore.

BIG BERTHA'S DAUGHTER. During the first few months of the war there was no large scale activity on the Western Front. Both sides used occasional artillery bursts to draw fire in order to obtain some indication of the opposing forces' artillery strength. The Germans used a number of big guns on railway mountings such as the one seen firing (above), reminiscent of the German "Big Berthas" of World War I fame. The mounting enabled the guns to be moved quickly from sector to sector. Most of the fighting in the European Theater at this time took place in the Saar-Moselle region.

GERMAN DEFENSE. Behind the Westwall of the Siegfried Line, Hitler and his associates planned the destruction of Europe while one of the most formidable defense systems ever devised stood guard. Barbed wire, tank obstacles and forts, ranging in depth to nine miles protected the avenues of entrance to Germany. Breaching the continuous line, from Switzerland to Saarbrucken and up through Aix-la-Chapelle on the Belgian border, would not be an easy task.

RIVER PLATTE BATTLE HEROES HONORED. On February
23, Londoners gave a tumultuous welcome to the officers and
men of the cruisers "Ajax" and "Exeter," victors of the battle
against the German pocket battleship "Admiral Graf Spee"
off Montevideo, Uruguay, in December, 1939. Rear Admiral
Harwood, Commander of the "Exeter," received the K.C.B.

Other officers and men who shared in the action were simi-
larly decorated. A royal investiture at the Horse Guard Pal-
ace was followed by a parade to the Guildhall where a cere-
monial luncheon took place in their honor. The picture (above)
shows the procession passing Admiralty Arch. Thousands had
jammed the sidewalks to cheer and pay tribute to their exploit.

FINNS AND RUSSIANS MEET AT HANGOE. After losing
Viborg, her most important port, Finland was forced to lease
the peninsula of Hangoe, key to the Gulf of Finland, to Russia.
The lease was to run for 30 years at yearly rental of about
$150,000. The evacuation of the ceded areas began on
March 14, 1940, and from Hangoe alone some 11,000 Finns
departed, taking with them what they were able to carry.
ABOVE. Three Russian soldiers face a Finnish sentry.

HITLER AND MUSSOLINI MEET. The meeting between the German and Italian dictators at Brenner on March 18 aroused world-wide speculation. It was reported from Rome that it was held in connection with a peace proposal of eleven points which Hitler had drawn up and shown to Sumner Welles. Mussolini, it was said, hoped to persuade the Fuehrer to modify them. It seems probable that the meeting was held to decide the role that Italy would play.

DENMARK AND NORWAY INVADED. The war, which had
become practically a war of nerves since October, 1939,
suddenly took a dramatic turn when in the early hours of
April 9, 1940, Germany invaded Norway and Denmark.
ABOVE. German troops are disembarking in Copenhagen
from one of the many ships which ferried them across the
Baltic. Meanwhile motorized units had invaded the country
from the south. Denmark was unable to do more than protest.
Hitler attempted to justify the action by claiming that
Britain and France were about to invade Scandinavia.

FIRST OF THE QUISLINGS. The occupation of Oslo, the capital of Norway, was a masterpiece of treachery. For months Germany had been scheming with a group of Norwegian traitors led by Major Vidkun Quisling. The invasion was brilliantly planned and executed. All strategic points were occupied simultaneously. The Norwegians, ill-prepared for resistance, were dazed by the speed of the occupation. UPPER. An anti-aircraft gunner scans the sky. LOWER. German tanks enter the city.

TRONDHEIM LANDING. Hitler, prepared to pay any price for the speedy capture of Norway, flung the German Navy recklessly into the struggle. Although the latter suffered severe losses from British submarines, surface vessels and planes (which sank several capital ships and destroyers), the move was successful. While the British Navy's attention was temporarily diverted, German troopships and transports carried men and munitions to Norway. ABOVE. Nazi troops head for shore after having disembarked from a heavy cruiser.

AID FOR NORWAY. The help which the British government had promised to Norway was not long in forthcoming. On April 15, it was announced that troops had made landings at several points and were establishing contact with Norwegian forces. The landing was accomplished without the loss of a single British ship or man, despite heavy attacks. UPPER. A troop transport steams into a Norwegian fjord. LOWER. Troops wearing their lifebelts stand on deck to await landing instructions.

HOLLAND INVADED. Shortly before dawn on Friday, May 10, the sleeping Holland countryside was roused by the drone of aircraft, and a full scale airborne invasion was under way. Parachutes floated to earth bearing the vanguard of Germany's army of paratroopers. They descended on Holland equipped with machine guns and portable radio transmitters, and established themselves in fields, behind dikes, and in empty houses to pave the way for troop-carrying planes.

BELGIUM INVADED. In addition to their thrusts into Holland and Luxemburg, the Germans crossed the Belgian frontier at four points on the morning of May 10. By demolishing bridges and rail lines, the Belgians managed to slow the enemy advance. Within a few hours after the attack, crack British and French troops rushed across the border to aid Belgium. UPPER. Nazi railroad repair men check the tracks for sabotage. LOWER. Enemy troops are ferried across a river.

THE UMBRELLA FOLDS. Confidence in the government led by Neville Chamberlain was seriously undermined by the general conduct of the war, and after a debate on the question in the House of Commons on May 8, Mr. Chamberlain invited members of the opposition to serve under him in a reconstructed cabinet. Labor, however, refused and on May 10, Mr. Chamberlain resigned and was succeeded by Winston Churchill (above), photographed outside No. 10 Downing Street, official residence of the Prime Minister. He is followed by Brenden Bracken, British Minister of Information. Mr. Churchill clutches his ubiquitous cigar and smiles.

HITLER'S BLITZKRIEG SLOWED. While the Belgian fortress of Liege still held out, the German attack southwest of the city pressed forward towards Brussels and the real and ultimate objective, northern France. This attack was slowed by the fierce resistance of Belgian troops, and the perpetual harassing of German columns by the R.A.F. When the Belgian troops withdrew, they destroyed bridges and means of communication. ABOVE. A German light tank is checked by a bridge that has been blown.

GERMANS PRESS HOME THE ATTACK IN BELGIUM. After crossing the Albert Canal on May 11, the Germans advanced towards Tongres and Waremme. Troops that had crossed the frontier farther north pushed southward with the eastern end of the Liege-Louvain-Brussels railway as their objective. The Belgian Army, which had taken up positions on the Meuse and the Albert Canal, was forced to fall back to a secondary line of defense after making an heroic stand against German mechanized units. UPPER. An advancing German column dashes across an exposed area. LOWER. German tanks advance along the shallow bed of a canal—an easier way to travel than over damaged or congested roads.

THE INVADERS HOIST THEIR FLAG. Brussels, the capital of Belgium, capitulated on May 17, after it had been blasted and scarred by terrific aerial attacks of high explosive and incendiary bombs. ABOVE. German soldiers are seen raising the Nazi standard over the captured city. For the second time within a quarter of a century, an enemy flag flew triumphantly over the Belgian metropolis. The enemy remained the same—merely its symbol had changed.

ACROSS THE AISNE. By May 20, the Germans were approaching Amiens, and farther east, advance detachments had reached the Aisne. Fully equipped to deal with all obstacles that might hinder their progress, they crossed the river on pontoon bridges, similar to that shown above, which could be rapidly erected. The speed with which the enemy succeeded in crossing France's water defenses was largely responsible for the early German advances.

GERMANS REACH THE CHANNEL. The Germans, capturing Amiens, Arras, and Abbeville, reached the sea on May 21, despite desperate Allied resistance. On the same day, they announced the capture of General Henri Honoré Giraud, Commander of the French Ninth Army, at Sedan. UPPER. The general arrives at a German airport as a prisoner. He escaped and rejoined the French command early in 1942. LOWER. British troops follow up a bombing attack.

BELGIUM SURRENDERS. A bitter blow was dealt to the Allied cause on May 28, when King Leopold of Belgium ordered his troops to cease fire, leaving the Allied left wing undefended. His order, repudiated by his Cabinet as unconstitutional, was obeyed by the bulk of his troops. UPPER. The king walks with his War Minister, General Denys, after the surrender. LOWER. Belgian troops seek shelter from an air raid on the last day of their participation in the war.

LUXEMBOURG INVADED. This little country, sandwiched between Belgium and France, stood in the path of the German war machine. With only a nominal army of some 250 men this small state was unable to do more than to raise an ineffectual protest against the Nazi aggressors. The invasion was timed to coincide with those conducted in Belgium and Holland. German motorcyclists are shown crossing into Luxembourg to meet French troops on hand to assist former.

THE HOURS OF CRISIS. On May 23 and 24 the German
Army reached the English Channel at Boulogne and Calais.
The collapse of Belgian resistance left the B.E.F. in Belgium
and northwest France in imminent danger of being surrounded
and driven into the sea. Attempts to rejoin the French Army
in the south were regarded as hopeless. The British were forced
to fight a delaying rear guard action and to attempt with-

drawal by sea. Weary British soldiers, harassed on all sides by
enemy fire, fell back towards Dunkirk. For many it was a continuous fighting march from the Luxemburg border. Equipment was abandoned and enemy fighters followed every step
of the way. A contingent of British troops (above) are seen
marching into the heavily bombed city. The evacuation has
been described as the most difficult in British history.

RESCUE BY SEA. Troops at Dunkirk scattered over the neighboring sand dunes, taking such cover as they could find, to avoid the relentless strafing from enemy planes. As the boats for evacuation were made available, the men waded and swam to meet their rescuers. This group of men, neck-deep in water, many still carrying their rifles and equipment, forms a human chain from ship to shore. Their buddies already aboard stand ready to assist them in their scramble up the ship's side.

THE UNCONQUERED. Every vessel afloat, capable of carrying men, was pressed into service to assist the British Navy's evacuation of Dunkirk. What could have been an overwhelming military victory for the German Army was turned into a moral victory for the British people. Although a great quantity of equipment was lost to the enemy, the British Army remained intact. Ships carrying the men home were continually strafed. ABOVE. Two destroyer-transports arrive in England.

THE "STAB IN THE BACK!" On 10 June, 1940, while France was at the last gasp of organized resistance against the Nazis, Italy declared war. After stabbing her in the back, Italy confined herself to air bombing of Malta, Alexandria, and Gibraltar. She invaded the southern part of France around the Alps just in time to join the hurrah and the spoils. Il Duce's troops which had beaten down the primitive Ethiopians were soon to make a sorry showing against Greece. Italy attempted to gain supremacy of the sea in the Mediterranean, but met with no degree of success. The British fleet tried to seek the Italians out and engage them in battle, but the Italian fleet remained in hiding and finally surrendered when Italy capitulated. Depicted (above) is a throng of Italian Fascists listening intently to their dictator, Benito Mussolini, reading the infamous Declaration of War against France in Rome.

NEW-TYPE SOLDIER. World War II saw the advent and use of many new types of weapons and of many unheard of methods of fighting. The airborne footsoldier, like the paratroopers preparing to jump (above), was among the more outstanding innovations. The 82nd and 101st Airborne Divisions landed behind the Germans at Normandy, the 11th Division helped rout the Japs on Leyte and Luzon, and other units made history wherever they fought.

ACTIVITY ON THE BEACH. UPPER. Hospital Corpsmen of the Navy Beach Battalion's Medical Section hit the beach with other sections to administer first aid to the wounded. LOWER. The beachmaster of a Navy Beach Battalion uses a "walkie-talkie" to maintain contact with other sections of his outfit. In the background other communications men are ready to use either blinker or signal flags on an invasion rehearsal in England.

PARIS OCCUPIED. By June 11, the battle for Paris reached
its peak. The city resisted but fell to the enemy on June
14. ABOVE. A German motorized unit passes the Obelisk.

END OF THE THIRD REPUBLIC. By Hitler's express orders, the stage set for the signing of the Franco-German armistice was exactly the same as on November 11, 1918, when Marshal Foch met the German plenipotentiaries on a similar errand. Then the armistice had been signed in a railway coach in the forest of Compiegne. Since 1918 that historic coach had been kept in the Invalides in Paris whence it had been moved after the Treaty of Versailles. Hitler ordered it to be taken to the exact spot in the forest where the act that had marked the cessation of hostilities in 1918 had taken place. Hitler could not have conceived a plan more humiliating to French pride than this resetting of the scene of her earlier triumph. The historical events depicted on these pages took place on the afternoon of June 21. UPPER RIGHT. The coach is being moved up into the exact position it occupied in 1918. UPPER LEFT. A German guard of honor marches around both the coach and the memorial to Germany's 1918 defeat. LOWER LEFT. Led by General Charles

Huntziger, the French delegates (left to right): Admiral Maurice Leluc, General Jean-Marie-Joseph Beregeret, and Leon Noel, in civilian attire, accompanied by the German officials arrive for the ceremony of the signature. The ceremony was brief. The preamble to the 32-page document was read, in German, by General Wilhelm Keitel, head of the German Supreme Command, and then in French. Hitler, who had said nothing during the proceedings, then left the others behind to study the terms of the agreement. LOWER RIGHT. Hitler is shown leaving the scene accompanied by General von Brauchitsch and Admiral Raeder on his right, and Herman Goering on his left. He is followed by Foreign Minister Joachim von Ribbentrop, and Rudolph Hess. General Keitel and General Huntziger, who voiced his protest at the severity of the terms, signed the document 27 hours later, in the early evening of June 22. After the armistice with Germany had been concluded, the French delegates left Compiegne and flew to Rome to conclude a similar armistice with Italy.

FIREMEN TACKLE THE FLAMES. On August 25, 1940,
shortly after midnight, the people of London were subjected
to their first aerial bombardment. LEFT. A fireman plays
a stream of water on a commercial building. ABOVE. Firemen watch as the last wisps of smoke rise from the wreckage.

ALL-NIGHT RAID ON BRITAIN'S CAPITAL. Goering's air force launched its first all-night raid on the British capital on August 26, 1940, when small waves of Nazi bombers operated repeatedly over the London area all through the night from 9:30 P.M. to 3:45 A.M. Though large quantities of bombs were dropped in residential districts over a wide area, the resultant damage was small and out of proportion to the "nuisance value" of the attack, the main purpose of which seemed to be the interruption of industrial production by depriving the workers of their sleep. The most illustrious victim claimed by the Nazis on this occasion was the poet, John Milton, whose statue outside the church where he is buried was blown from its pedestal and slightly damaged by a bomb blast. ABOVE. Searchlights, blazing from the blacked out city, flamboyantly sweep the heavens in search of the marauders.

SURVEYING THE DAMAGE. Londoners subsequently grew accustomed to the nightly visits of the German Air Force, and stoically accepted the devastation that greeted them daily on their way to work. Scenes like the one (above) showing scarred buildings along the approach to London Bridge were common throughout the British capital. The attacks, instead of reducing industrial production, only provoked the people into surpassing their previous records.

ITALIAN ULTIMATUM REJECTED. In May, 1940, Italy advised the Greek government that "should Italy be involved in a war against Great Britain, she would not attack Greece, provided the latter was not converted into a British base." Then, on October 28, 1940, Italy, alleging violation of Greek neutrality, presented a three-hour ultimatum to Greece, demanding that certain unspecified strategic points be conceded. The Greek Premier, General Metaxas, considered the ultimatum a declaration of war. Within two and a half hours after delivery of the ultimatum, Italian troops crossed the Greek-Albanian border. Italians remained unaware they were at war with Greece until October 29, when radio Rome announced that Italian troops had penetrated forty miles into Greece. UPPER LEFT. Greek troops stand guard at the frontier. ABOVE. Greek soldiers fasten their sights on the approaching enemy. LOWER LEFT. Members of the Italian cavalry ride into Greece. BELOW. Greek warships patrol the coastline.

ITALIAN ADVANCE HALTED. The Italian thrust into Greece toward Salonika was contained within three miles of the frontier, and within a few days counter-attacking Greek troops, intent on the annihilation of the invaders, hurled the enemy back into Albania. By November 5, Koritza was within range of Greek artillery. Meanwhile, two Italian attacks designed to encircle Yanina were brought to a standstill. On November 11, the Greeks announced their first victory, the capture of the bulk of a reinforced mountain division of Alpine troops in the northern sector. This move marked the beginning of a general advance of the Greek Army which culminated in 1941 with the entire coast of Albania in Greek hands. Two thousand Greek soldiers had accomplished the impossible—they had contained the Italians and forced them into full retreat. UPPER LEFT. Italian troops in complete rout, their mechanized transport abandoned, urge on a mule team. LOWER LEFT. Engineers build a temporary bridge. UPPER RIGHT. Tanks captured by the Greeks. LOWER RIGHT. Captured Italian mortars.

AFTER THE RAID. The German radio, gloating over the havoc
wrought in Coventry by their bombers coined a new word,
"Coventrated," to describe what their air force had done to
the city. Although buildings on both sides of the street were

gutted, the familiar town clock remained unscathed. The spirit of the people of Coventry may best be judged from the mayor's remark on seeing the damage (above): "We've always wanted a site for a new civic center and now we have it."

LONDON GUTTED. Christmas brought a lull in the aerial war over Great Britain. Shortly after dark on the evening of December 29, waves of raiders, flying over the heart of the city, rained thousands of incendiary and explosive bombs on the historic buildings, in a deliberate effort to surpass the effects of the Great Fire of 1666. St. Paul's, close-ringed by flame, remained practically unharmed; but many of Sir Christopher Wren's famous churches were reduced to ashes. It was a battered London to which workers returned the morning after the raid. Miles of hose lay tangled everywhere. UPPER LEFT. The steeple of St. Paul's viewed from the ruined archway of a smouldering building. ABOVE. Fire fighting equipment which was destroyed in the blaze. UPPER RIGHT. Firemen battle a stubborn fire along a main thoroughfare of the city. LEFT. Office workers climb over hoses on their way to work. RIGHT. Firemen and soldiers continue their work.

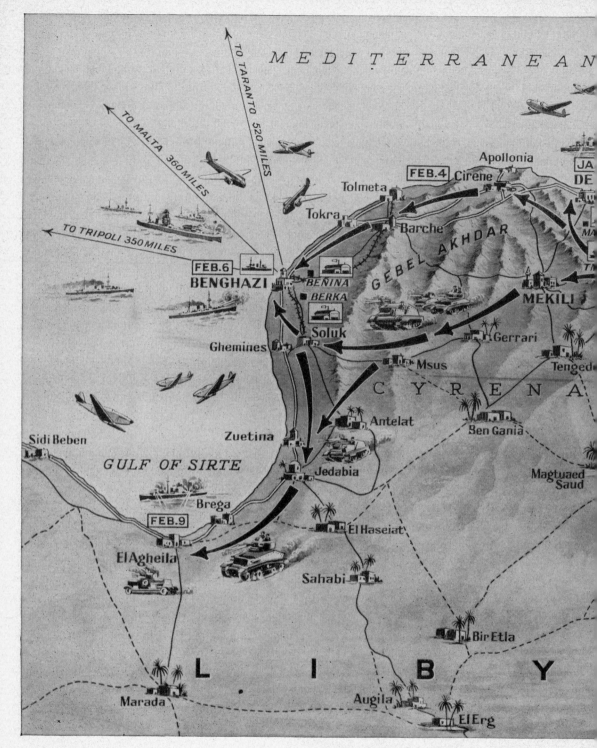

BRITAIN'S CONQUEST OF EASTERN LIBYA. The brilliant forward movement along the coast of Italian North Africa, begun on December 9, 1940, and culminating in the capture of Benghazi on February 6, 1941, was acclaimed as one of the most brilliant campaigns in military history. The Army of the Nile, consisting of approximately 30,000 men, advanced within two months more than 500 miles through practically roadless and waterless country, with ever-lengthening lines of communi-

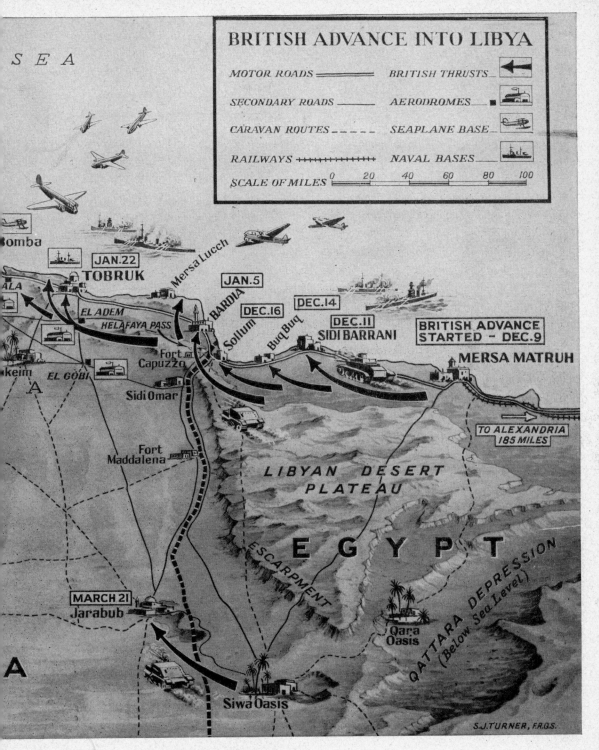

BRITISH ADVANCE INTO LIBYA

MOTOR ROADS —————	BRITISH THRUSTS
SECONDARY ROADS ———	AERODROMES
CARAVAN ROUTES – – – –	SEAPLANE BASE
RAILWAYS +++++++++++	NAVAL BASES
SCALE OF MILES 0 20 40 60 80 100	

SEA

Bomba

Mersa Lucch

JAN.22 TOBRUK

ALA

EL ADEM
HELAFAYA PASS

BARDIA

JAN.5

DEC.16

DEC.14

BuqBuq

DEC.11
SIDI BARRANI

BRITISH ADVANCE
STARTED – DEC.9

MERSA MATRUH

keim EL GOBI

Fort
Capuzzo

Sidi Omar

Sollum

A

TO ALEXANDRIA
185 MILES

Fort
Maddalena

LIBYAN DESERT
PLATEAU

E G Y P T

ESCARPMENT

MARCH 21
Jarabub

Qara
Oasis

QATTARA DEPRESSION
(Below Sea Level)

A

Siwa Oasis

S.J.TURNER, F.R.G.S.

cation. They captured approximately 140,000 prisoners, including 19 enemy generals, plus vast quantities of war
materiel of all kinds, at a cost of only about 2,000 British
casualties. During the earlier stages great assistance was
afforded the land army by naval supporting forces, and the
success was also due in great measure to the air superiority
early established by the R.A.F. The map (above) depicts
pictorially and in detail the various stages of the advance.

ASSAULT ON TOBRUK. The battle of Tobruk followed the lines previously employed at Bardia, the town being attacked simultaneously from several points. By encircling the enemy positions, the attackers were able to take Italian forces in the rear, thereby throwing them into confusion and making them face both ways at once. Allied casualties were very light, less than 500 in all; nearly 20,000 Italian prisoners

were taken as well as many guns and large stores of materiel.
UPPER LEFT. A British medium howitzer is fired during the
preliminary bombardment. UPPER RIGHT. British infantry
make their way through barbed wire defenses outside the
town. LOWER. Men of the Australian Imperial forces advance
toward their objective supported by light tanks. They are disposed in open formation as a precaution against air attack.

ROYAL NAVY POUNDS GENOA. In an early morning bombardment by the British Mediterranean Fleet on February 9, 1941, more than three hundred tons of shells were rained on the harbor. Many important objectives, including the main power station, the Ansaldo electrical and boiler works, oil fuel installations, and several supply ships, were repeatedly hit. UPPER. A view of the Italian naval base at Genoa. LOWER. the British battleship "Renown" in action.

FATE OF GERMAN U-BOATS. With the advent of spring, 1941, the Nazi campaign against British and Allied shipping was intensified with the total losses to U-Boats amounting to approximately 225 ships with tonnage of about 500,000 tons. Measures against the raiders were stepped up considerably with the certain destruction of several announced in March. UPPER. The last member of a German submarine about to jump. LOWER. The crew after it had abandoned ship.

LADY ASTOR'S CONSTITUENCY HIT. Nazi bombers made Plymouth their main target in two particularly heavy night raids toward the end of March, 1941. The destruction wrought by the attacks was officially stated to be at least as heavy as any provincial city had thus far sustained in air attacks. The "military objectives" hit included dwellings, shops, churches, theaters, and hotels, and the casualties were heavy. In the second raid, the more severe of the two, more than 20,000

incendiary bombs were dropped along with the high explosives. These were followed by sustained dive bombing and
machine gun attacks on the ruins. However, on both nights,
serious fires were soon brought under control by the local firefighting services who stayed at their posts in spite of the
ferocity of the bombardment. LEFT. One of the bombed areas
of a business district in Plymouth. RIGHT. Churchill, then
Prime Minister, is welcomed by workmen as he tours the city.

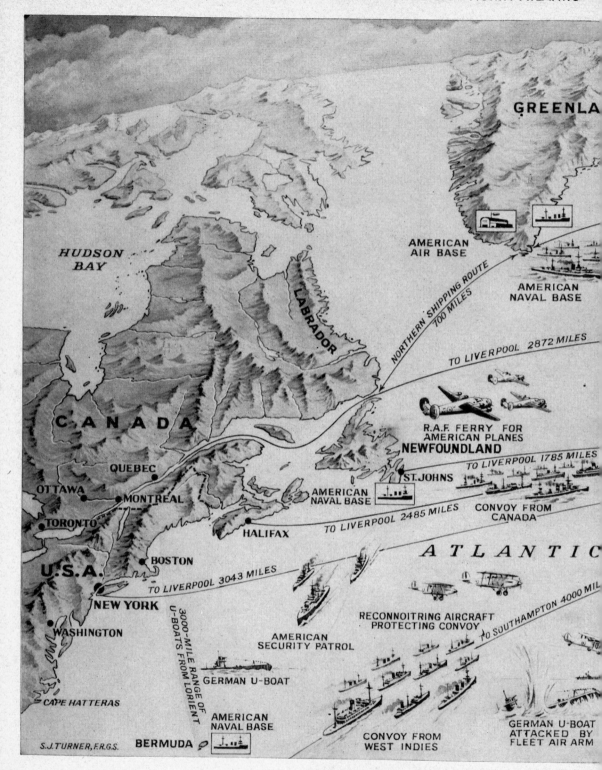

GREENLA

AMERICAN
AIR BASE

AMERICAN
NAVAL BASE

HUDSON
BAY

LABRADOR

NORTHERN SHIPPING ROUTE 700 MILES

TO LIVERPOOL 2872 MILES

R.A.F. FERRY FOR
AMERICAN PLANES

NEWFOUNDLAND

TO LIVERPOOL 1785 MILES

C A N A D A

QUEBEC

OTTAWA

MONTREAL

ST. JOHNS

AMERICAN
NAVAL BASE

CONVOY FROM
CANADA

TORONTO

TO LIVERPOOL 2485 MILES

HALIFAX   A T L A N T I C

U.S.A.

BOSTON

TO LIVERPOOL 3043 MILES

NEW YORK

3000-MILE RANGE OF
U-BOATS FROM LORIENT

WASHINGTON

RECONNOITRING AIRCRAFT
PROTECTING CONVOY

TO SOUTHAMPTON 4000 MIL

AMERICAN
SECURITY PATROL

GERMAN U-BOAT

CAPE HATTERAS

AMERICAN
NAVAL BASE

S. J. TURNER, F.R.G.S.   BERMUDA

CONVOY FROM
WEST INDIES

GERMAN U-BOAT
ATTACKED BY
FLEET AIR ARM

BATTLE OF THE ATLANTIC. Adolph Hitler's ominous boast
that, with the coming of spring, 1941, German U-Boat and
aerial warfare against Britiain's convoys in the Atlantic would
be intensified, constituted no idle threat. In March and April
of that year, the British and Allied shipping losses rose to
approximately 500,000 tons representing in all a staggering

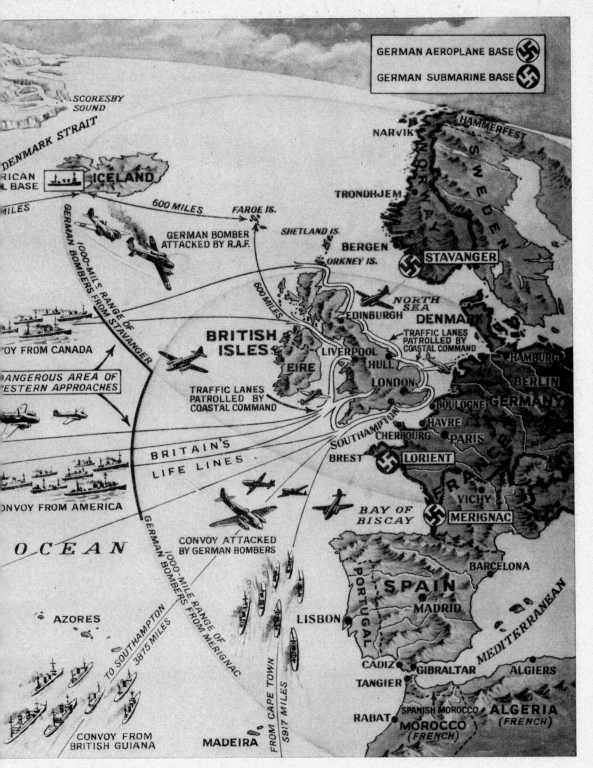

GERMAN AEROPLANE BASE

GERMAN SUBMARINE BASE

SCORESBY SOUND

DENMARK STRAIT

RICAN L BASE

ICELAND

600 MILES

FAROE IS.

GERMAN BOMBER ATTACKED BY R.A.F.

SHETLAND IS.

NARVIK

HAMMERFEST

TRONDHJEM

BERGEN

ORKNEY IS.

STAVANGER

600 MILES

NORTH SEA

EDINBURGH

DENMARK

TRAFFIC LANES PATROLLED BY COASTAL COMMAND

1000-MILE RANGE OF GERMAN BOMBERS FROM STAVANGER

BRITISH ISLES

EIRE

LIVERPOOL

HULL

LONDON

HAMBURG

BERLIN

GERMANY

OY FROM CANADA

DANGEROUS AREA OF ESTERN APPROACHES

TRAFFIC LANES PATROLLED BY COASTAL COMMAND

SOUTHAMPTON

CHERBOURG

HAVRE

PARIS

BOULOGNE

BRITAIN'S LIFE LINES

ONVOY FROM AMERICA

BREST

LORIENT

FRANCE

VICHY

MERIGNAC

BAY OF BISCAY

OCEAN

CONVOY ATTACKED BY GERMAN BOMBERS

1000-MILE RANGE OF GERMAN BOMBERS FROM MERIGNAC

BARCELONA

AZORES

PORTUGAL

SPAIN

MADRID

MEDITERRANEAN

TO SOUTHAMPTON 3875 MILES

LISBON

CADIZ

GIBRALTAR

ALGIERS

TANGIER

FROM CAPE TOWN 5917 MILES

SPANISH MOROCCO

ALGERIA (FRENCH)

RABAT

CONVOY FROM BRITISH GUIANA

MADEIRA

MOROCCO (FRENCH)

total of 225 ships. In spite of all the enemy could do, however, Britiain's lifeline, although stretched, remained unbroken due to the heroic efforts of both the British Fleet and the R.A.F. The map (above) depicts the routes taken by convoys from America and Canada, along with the measures employed to outwit both the enemy's submarines and long-range bombers.

BATTLE OF THE ATLANTIC

By Admiral Jonas H. Ingram, USN

MORE than two years before the formal entry of the United States into World War II, the Atlantic Fleet began to support the British Fleet. This was done by the Neutrality Patrol, established in September 1939.

Fifteen months before the Japanese attack on Pearl Harbor, fifty Atlantic Fleet destroyers were turned over to Great Britain in exchange for base rights, and the rapid development of the outposts during 1941 permitted the Atlantic Fleet to prepare a series of valuable stepping stones for wartime operations. Another vital extension of our defenses occurred in May 1941 when Brazil authorized the Atlantic Fleet to build and use advanced bases for planes and surface craft at Recife, Bahia, and Natal.

Aggressively committed to the task of maintaining the war-making capacity of the British Isles, the United States could not afford to let German submarines sink lend-lease supplies en route, and the Atlantic Fleet joined British and Canadian naval forces during the summer of 1941, with orders to "shoot on sight" at any ships, planes or submarines which threatened this steady flow of war materials through the Western Atlantic.

By the time the attack on Pearl Harbor occurred, the Atlantic Fleet had already completed and had begun to use a destroyer base in Londonderry, Ireland. In the far-flung struggle to maintain convoy lanes which soon stretched from the United Kingdom to Halifax, New York, Trinidad, Aruba, Recife, and Rio de Janeiro, Admiral Doenitz's ruthless offensive maintained a decided edge. But in May 1943, Allied team-work with long-range planes, surface ships and baby flat tops succeeded in sinking 43 U-boats, and this stunning defeat was the climax of the Battle of the Atlantic. Thereafter, the initiative in that phase of the conflict passed to the Allies and was never again lost.

SUPPORTING THE EUROPEAN LANDINGS

CLOSELY interlocked with the submarine war were the overseas movements of great armadas to launch those major amphibious operations which led to the final defeat of the Axis: the landings in North Africa, the Sicilian and Italian campaigns, and the invasions of Normandy and Southern France. To assist the British and Canadians in all of these difficult tasks, the Amphibious Force of the Atlantic Fleet provided extensive training to our Army troops. The important part played by Atlantic Fleet ships in transporting these specially trained troops, in landing them successfully on

hostile shores, and in supporting their initial assaults, won the grudging praise of an enemy who had never understood the importance of true function of sea power.

All of these landings required preliminary build-up of supplies and subsequent feeding of additional materials and troops from the United States—responsibilities which continued to be taken by units of the Atlantic Fleet. Shipments for the initial invasion of Normandy alone piled up more than 16,000,000 tons of supplies in Britain during one year before D-day.

Another important aspect of the Battle of the Atlantic was the Allied campaign against blockade runners which shuttled high priority minerals and rubber from Japan to Germany, high grade steel and precision instruments from Germany to Japan. During 1941 and 1942, the enemy sent out 49 blockade-running freighters or tankers from Europe, and 40 of them made the round trip successfully. An Allied "barrier" of ships and planes across the narrows of the South Atlantic (greatly strengthened by our Army-Navy air base on Ascension) was gradually developed to maximum efficiency toward the end of 1943 and the beginning of 1944. Climax of this "barrier" strategy was achieved during the first week of 1944, when planes and surface craft of the Atlantic Fleet's South Atlantic Force pulled off a triple play and sank three blockade runners in three consecutive days. Forced to abandon such costly and fruitless endeavors, the enemy resorted to using his largest supply-submarines, and again suffered heavy losses. The only Japanese submarine sunk in the Atlantic was one of these supply-submarines, loaded with raw rubber, which was nailed by coordinated attacks of an Atlantic Fleet killer group built around a baby flat top and operating south of the Azores.

Final tabulations revealed that 126 enemy submarines were sunk by Atlantic Fleet units. On the defensive side of the ledger, Atlantic Fleet ships escorted 17,707 ships in convoy, of which only 17 were sunk and 14 damaged by enemy action. As the Battle of the Atlantic drew to successful conclusion, more than 800 ships, trained in the Atlantic Fleet, passed through the Panama Canal to join forces in the Pacific between 1 January and 16 May 1945.

GERMAN PLAN FOR BALKANS FOILED. Consternation at the news that Yugoslavian Premier M. Tsvetkovich had signed a Vienna treaty to align his country with the Axis fired a revolution in protest to the move. At midnight, on March 26, 1941, the revolution broke out, led by General Simovich, who later became premier. In the picture (upper), M. Tsvetkovich (center) and his foreign minister, M. Cincar-Markovich, take leave of Joachim von Ribbentrop at Salzburg after a conference with Hitler in February. LOWER. A student demonstration takes place in Belgrade after the coup.

ABYSSINIAN CAPITAL RECOVERED. South African troops
ended an Italian domination over Ethiopia lasting five years
when on April 5, they entered the capital after an advance
of 700 miles. The maneuver took 27 days. The city was surrendered by the Italians without resistance. The Italian viceroy,
the Duke of Aosta, and part of the garrison, had already with-

drawn when the South Africans reached the city. ABOVE. A
Transvaal regiment, headed by its pipers, marches through
the streets of the liberated town accompanied by delighted
Abyssinians, who had been held in virtual slavery by the
Italians. On the fifth anniversary of the entry of Italian
troops into the city, Haile Selassie, the Emperor, returned.

ATTACK ON OPEN YUGOSLAV CAPITAL. The German on-slaught on Yugoslavia began with a damaging air raid on Belgrade, April 6. The raid was made despite the fact that the city had been declared open. Three additional attacks took place during the day, rivaling in ferocity earlier raids on Warsaw and Rotterdam. Although the small Yugoslav air force gallantly attacked the superior enemy formations, thousands were killed, and much of the city ruined. LEFT. An aerial view of part of the devastated city. RIGHT. Nazi tanks pass General von Kleist after occupying city, April 12.

FIRST DAY OF BALKAN ADVANCE. Germany attacked
Greece through the Rupel Pass into the Struma Valley, leading from Bulgaria into Greece. Their aim was to seize Salonika and cut off the Greek troops in eastern Thrace from
their main body. UPPER. A Nazi motorized unit protected by
anti-aircraft. LOWER. Germans haul an 8-8 cm. gun across a
Balkan River over a hastily-erected pontoon bridge.

THIS WAS IT! ABOVE. Invasion troops embarking in England for the Normandy invasion. Hitler had boasted that the Atlantic coast of France was impregnable, that all Europe was a Fascist fortress. Well, they would see! Rehearsals had ended when this picture was made—and this was it! Early on the morning of June 6, 1944, began the greatest amphibious operation in the history of the world. At long last the combined might of the Allied world was ready to strike, and it struck before dawn. Crossing the Channel in a gigantic fleet of more than 4,000 ships and boats, including 800 warships, the invaders landed on five beaches. In the American sector the beach areas totaled 10,000 yards in length. Every 75 yards a landing craft touched down at H-Hour. Resistance was fierce as Marshal Rommel sought to roll up the beachhead. But he failed, and the invaders proved Hitler's boast was empty.

DANGEROUS DUTY. The advantage of the airborne infantryman was that he could be dropped behind enemy lines to disrupt communications, gain valuable intelligence and create general confusion. Often during the war—the Battle of the Bulge is a good example—they landed in strategic areas to reinforce hard-pressed troops. Their duty was nearly always extremely dangerous. ABOVE. Paratroopers on patrol ski over the snow-blanketed hills of the French Alps.

U-BOAT CAPTAINS EXCHANGE FAREWELLS. The British announced that although many U-Boats had been sunk leaving no survivors, about 500 German officers and men from other sunken submarines had been rescued and made prisoners. Among them was Commander Otto Kretschmer, U-Boat ace, decorated by Hitler in August, 1940. Another noted Commander, Captain Schepke, went down with his ship in April. The picture (above) shows Captain Schutze, a third Nazi hero, saying farewell before leaving for a raiding cruise.

NAZIS IN ATHENS. Though Athens itself was not the victim of air attack by the Germans, its suburbs were a target for the "Luftwaffe" on April 22 and 25. ABOVE. German infantry marching through Athens. UPPER and LOWER LEFT. German and Italian motorized detachments pass in formation during a review following the occupation.

DESTRUCTION FROM ABOVE. On the night of April 16, a force of more than 500 German bombers attacked London in what was said to be the most destructive raid of the war. Most of the damage was done by fire, the Nazis claiming that more than 100,000 incendiary bombs were dropped. Hospitals, churches, homes and other non-military objectives suffered most. This photograph of a blazing building in the heart of the city was taken at the height of the blitz.

FIRST CALM—THEN THE STORM. On the full-moon night of May 10, after an almost raid-free three weeks, London endured an intense air attack lasting for several hours, resulting in many casualties and heavy destruction. Large numbers of incendiaries were dropped along with the usual high explosive bombs, and among those killed were the mayors of two London boroughs. Both Houses of Parliament were damaged, and the Commons' debating chamber was wrecked.

FRANCO-GERMAN PACT. On May 6, Admiral Darlan and Herr Abetz, German representative in France, signed an agreement providing for certain "concessions" in the occupation terms. On May 15 the French authorities allowed German planes to use Syrian airfields. The picture (upper) shows the men of Vichy at a ministerial council. Marshal Petain, the Premier, is shown to the left of the picture, and seated opposite him is Admiral Darlan, who negotiated the agreement with the Nazis. LOWER. The Marshal greets a crowd.

NUMBER THREE NAZI BAILS OUT. The world was astounded to learn on May 12 that Rudolf Hess, Deputy Fuehrer of Germany, had landed near Glasgow by parachute after flying from Germany in a Messerschmitt 110. No official explanation of his desertion was made, but the general view was that Hess' flight indicated a serious breach of solidarity in the Nazi party, possibly on the question of Russo-German relations. UPPER. Hess, in cockpit, is bidding goodbye to his wife before a flight. LOWER. The wreck of the escape plane.

THE "HOOD" REVENGED. In a naval engagement on May 24, 1941, Germany's newest and largest battleship, the "Bismarck," sunk H.M.S. "Hood." On the same day, with her speed somewhat reduced, the former was attacked and hit by planes from the aircraft carrier "Victorious." Early on the morning of the 25th contact was lost. Other British units joined in the chase, assisted by R.A.F. planes, and the "Bismarck" was again located 550 miles west of Land's End on May 26. Planes from H.M.S. "Ark Royal" attacked her twice in the

afternoon, scoring hits and further reducing her speed. On the morning of the 27th, culminating a chase that had covered 1,750 miles, the "Bismarck" was finally sunk by a torpedo from H.M.S. "Dorsetshire." The original intention to sink her by gunfire was abandoned owing to poor visibility. LEFT. The "Bismarck" just before the fatal torpedoes were launched. UPPER RIGHT. Members of her crew struggling in the water. LOWER RIGHT. This picture, taken from a ship of the Royal Navy, reveals the "Bismarck" aflame in the background.

ON TO MOSCOW! Flushed with easy victories over Poland, France, and the Low Countries, and the Balkans, Hitler suddenly turned treacherously on Russia whom he thought he had deceived with one of his false peace pacts. On June 22, 1941, he began an all out attack on the greatest scale ever yet conceived by man. With between 150 and 180 divisions in the surprise attack, the Germans counted on a quick capture of Moscow and the Caucasus. UPPER. German grenadiers waving a swastika flag to show Stuka pilots their positions so they would not bomb their own lines. LOWER. German tanks and half-tracks advancing on a Soviet position in a thrust on the Orel-Belgorod sector. Both of the pictures depicted above are confiscated German Army photographs.

MINSK FALLS TO ADVANCING NAZIS. The most successful of the German thrusts into Russia took place in the central sector against Moscow. The Germans fought one of the greatest tank battles of the war here with 4,000 tanks participating. On June 26, the Nazis broke the Russian defenses, and four days later announced the capture of Minsk. The Russian plan was to allow the enemy mechanized spearheads to penetrate their lines and then to close the gap and isolate the fighting vehicles from the supporting infantry.

RUSSIAN "PANZER" DIVISIONS. The U.S.S.R., which had
for years been successfully mechanizing its army with an eye
to possible German attack, met the onslaught of the Nazi
Panzer divisions with an armored force equal in strength to
that of the attacker. UPPER. Red tanks moving up to the
front through heavily-wooded country; they are camouflaged
with branches of trees as a safeguard against observation
or bombing attack. LOWER. Russian officers of a tank column
conferring at the front before probing new terrain.

ALLIES TAKE PALMYRA. British and Free French troops closed in on the ruined desert city of Palmyra on the 26th of June. The city, important strategically for its oil pipeline to Tripoli, was stubbornly defended by Vichy troops who had even hired Arab snipers to stem Allied advances. However, they were forced to retire, and on July 3 the allied troops took over. ABOVE. A Bren gun carrier amid the ruins of the old Roman Colonnade. The crew dismounts to deal with remaining pockets of resistance in the North African city.

BRITAIN AND U.S.S.R. BECOME ALLIES. On July 9, 1941, a Russian mission arrived in London to discuss common action to be taken against Germany. UPPER. M. Maisky, Soviet Ambassador, with General Golikov (light tunic), Rear Admiral Kharlamov (behind him), and other members of the mission on their arrival. Four days later in Moscow, Sir Stafford Cripps, British Ambassador to the U.S.S.R. (lower), signed a treaty of mutual assistance.

THE "V FOR VICTORY" SIGN. During a conversation with Prime Minister Churchill during their momentous Atlantic Charter meeting on August 10, 1941, President Roosevelt's fingers form the British victory sign. The Charter was part of America's answer to the Tripartite Pact signed by Germany, Italy, and Japan in September, 1940, which threatened combined Axis action against any neutral which should interfere with Axis aggressions. The United States had already challenged that threat by its Lend-Lease aid, its occupation of Iceland to forestall possible German invasion, and its naval patrol of northern hemispheric waters east to Greenland. The Axis dictators should have recognized the importance of the Charter Meeting. ABOVE. In addition to the President and the British Premier, the meeting included Fleet Admiral Ernest J. King, General of the Army George C. Marshall, and British General Sir John Dill.

GERMANS FIND KIEV AFLAME. UPPER LEFT. A party of
German troops assault a Russian position on the outskirts of
the city. LOWER LEFT. Buildings in the center of the
Ukrainian capital left blazing by the retreating Russians.
RIGHT. German soldiers in one of Kiev's main thoroughfares.

MOSCOW WITHSTANDS NAZI SURGE. The third German
drive towards Moscow began on October 1, 1941, with pincer
thrusts in the Roslavl and Kholm areas. By the 7th the enemy
were in Orel exerting heavy pressure near Bryansk and
Vyazma. The two towns capitulated on the 12th and 13th respectively. Two days later a German column penetrated as
far as Mojaisk, but was driven back by a well-timed counter-
attack. The Russians realizing the seriousness of the situation,

admitted that the Germans were using about 18,000 tanks on this front alone. On the 19th, after the fall of Kalinin and Kaluga, Stalin issued an order declaring that the city of Moscow would defend itself to the last man. UPPER LEFT. Russian prisoners captured during the fighting at Bryansk. LOWER LEFT. Men of the Hitler Corps passing through a burnt-out village. UPPER RIGHT. Women and children seeking safety. LOWER RIGHT. A German tank in Vyazma.

TOMAHAWKS TO THE RESCUE. The tank battle of Sidi Rezegh continued until November 28, 1941, when there was a pause. During this time, General Rommel, the famed Desert Fox, had been trying unsuccessfully to break through the British ring. Sidi Rezegh, itself, changed hands several times. Meanwhile, New Zealand infantry, pushing westward along the coast, occupied Bardia on the 22nd, Gambut on the 23rd, and on the 27th linked up at El Duda with a force that had sallied forth from Tobruk. In succeeding days these troops

gradually widened their corridor, but on the 29th the Sidi
Rezegh battle flared up once again. After several more unsuccessful attempts to break through to the west, Rommel
finally concentrated all his available tanks on a narrow front,
and on December I succeeded in hammering his way through
the Tobruk corridor by sheer weight of armor. Both the R.A.F.
and the R.A.A.F. play prominent roles in these operations
bombing enemy communications and harassing ground forces.
The fighter pilots (above) are Aussies using American planes.

GERMAN ATTACK BOGS DOWN. Hitler's bid to take Moscow continued unabated throughout October and November with the "Wehrmacht" making slow progress. Then, in December, the Germans threw every available man and tank into a gigantic frontal attack. Advance units penetrated to within thirty miles of the capital but progressed no farther. With the advent of winter the Russians took the initiative. UPPER LEFT. Citizens dig anti-tank ditches. LOWER LEFT. Cossacks attack an enemy position near the city. UPPER RIGHT. German soldiers retreat north of Moscow. LOWER RIGHT. Russian tank en route to front.

GERMANS RETREAT BEFORE MOSCOW. After bringing the
German offensive to a standstill, the defenders of Moscow
launched a series of strong counter-attacks all along the line.
By December 15, 1941, they had recaptured several major
cities. UPPER. Guns and vehicles abandoned by Germans during a retreat. LOWER. Russians advance through a town.

RECAPTURE OF TIKHVIN. Although the Germans succeeded in encircling Leningrad, their efforts to take it by storm failed. Nevertheless, during October and November, they did push slowly eastward and on November 29 captured Tikhvin, 100 miles southeast of the city. On December 8, however, Russian forces under General Merezhkov re-entered Tikhvin after a battle in which more than 7,000 German soldiers were killed. At about this time, the crisis in Russia induced the U.S. to aid here. UPPER. German horse-transport units in retreat. LOWER. Russian infantry supporting a tank attack.

HITLER SIGNS HIS OWN DEATH WARRANT. With the triumphant reports of the Japanese after Pearl Harbor still ringing in his ears, Chancellor Hitler stood in the Reichstag and launched the German state into the war with the United States that was to cost the Nazis all that they had already won. Although sure of victory he bombastically announced that he would give his life, if necessary, for the German cause, and that in that case Marshal Herman Goering (seated directly above him) would be his successor. ABOVE. The scene in the Reichstag as Hitler announced to the German nation that the Third Reich was officially at war with the United States.

AT WAR WITH GERMANY AND ITALY. On December 11, 1941, thinking that their Japanese Allies had destroyed United States sea power in their treacherous Pearl Harbor attack, Germany and Italy also declared war on the United States. On that same day Congress unanimously recognized the state of war thrust upon us. Just as unanimously did the people of the United States take up the challenge. Volunteers swarmed to recruiting offices, training stations expanded a hundred fold; shipyards, munitions plants, airplane factories grew overnight. ABOVE. The picture shows President Roosevelt at his desk in the White House signing the war resolution of Congress.

SIEGE OF SEVASTOPOL. After capturing Feodosia, the German forces in the Crimea drove eastward and, on November 16, captured the town of Kerch thereby compelling the Russians to carry out a hazardous withdrawal across the Kerch Straits. Meanwhile, on the west of the Crimea, the Germans had thrown 3 armored and 9 infantry divisions against the defenses of the Russian naval base at Sevastopol. Yet the Russians did not yield and tremendous losses resulted to the attackers. ABOVE. Parents have just found the body of their son, a victim of the battle, among other bodies strewn about.

AXIS GARRISONS SURRENDER. The town of Bardia, which had been occupied by New Zealanders on November 22, and reoccupied by the enemy on December 1, surrendered unconditionally to British and Imperial forces on January 2, after a brilliant attack in which Polish and Free French forces took part. Having reduced Bardia, the British forces turned to remaining pockets of resistance in E. Cyrenaica. On the 12th they captured Sollum; on the 17th, Helafaya. UPPER. Prisoners captured at Sollum. LOWER. Axis surrenders at Helafaya.

ATTEMPT TO RELIEVE LENINGRAD. On February 23, the twenty-fourth anniversary of the creation of the Russian Army, Red forces launched an offensive on the Central Front, and on the same day the High Command announced the capture of Dorogobuzh, fifty miles east of Smolensk. Farther north, where the Russians were striving to break the German ring around Leningrad, Soviet troops, on the 24th, successfully accomplished the encirclement of the German 16th Army at Staraya

Russa, ten miles south of Lake Ilmen. After the German commander's refusal to surrender, the Soviets began an attack in which two German infantry divisions and the crack S.S. "Death's Head" Division were smashed with 12,000 Germans killed. Nevertheless, the enemy, heartened by promises of airborne reinforcements, clung desperately to their positions. LEFT. German infantrymen wait in the snow beside their guns. RIGHT. Russian sappers clear a path through enemy wire.

AFTERMATH OF BATTLE. On March 24, 1942, the Germans launched the biggest attack on the Kalinin front since the abortive Battle of Moscow. Its object was to relieve a salient in their lines near Rzhev, where two large bodies of Nazi troops had been isolated. For this purpose they employed three divisions and large numbers of tanks and aircraft, but after five days' fighting they were obliged to call off the attack. Death had cut down 2,500 of them. Near Staraya Russa, the Germans were still trying to relieve their Sixteenth Army which

had now been reduced by almost half. On the Leningrad front the Red Army was trying to free the encircled city before the thaw cut the supply line across the ice on Lake Ladoga, while in the Ukraine they had reached the suburbs of Stalino, which they had lost on October 20, and were fighting desperately to regain possession of the town. ABOVE. A Russian battlefield after the tide of war receded is etched with death. Bodies and burnt-out tanks litter the ground. Scenes such as this were typical throughout the length and breadth of the ETO.

MALTA DEFIES THE "LUFTWAFFE." The island of Malta,
which stands on the direct sea route from Italy to North
Africa, and from which attacks were carried out by British
aircraft on Axis convoys carrying reinforcements to General
Rommel in Libya, was the target of almost non-stop attacks
by German and Italian bombers. During April, 1942, the enemy launched a particularly heavy offensive in order to
ground British aircraft while his convoys made the crossing to
North Africa. On April 7, Malta had its two thousandth alert

since the war began. On this day alone the enemy employed about 500 aircraft in attacks on the island. According to reports from Valetta, the capital, about 4,200 homes had been destroyed in raids to date, as well as the island's Opera House, the Church and Monastery of the Sacred Heart, the Capuchin Convent Church, and the Chapel of Our Lady of Lourdes. LEFT. Devastation in Valetta. UPPER RIGHT. Bombs burst in the harbor area. LOWER RIGHT. A burst on the island in another of the relentless attacks.

GERMANS RELIEVE 16TH ARMY. On April 24, the Germans succeeded in relieving their Sixteenth Army which had been encircled near Staraya Russa, in February. During the two months it had been cut off, it had been kept supplied by air, and although its ranks had been seriously depleted, it had nevertheless remained intact as a fighting unit. ABOVE. German soldiers walk from their dugouts and surrender. The dead bodies of their comrades in the foreground bear witness to the doggedness of their resistance, and their confidence in the promise, made by the German High Command, of relief.

START OF THE GERMAN DRIVE. On May 8, German and
Rumanian forces, under General von Manstein, launched
a limited local offensive in the Crimea with the object of
clearing that area of Russian troops and safeguarding their
right flank against any possible Russian attack. In the face
of very strong pressure, the Soviet forces slowly withdrew,
inflicting heavy casualties on the enemy as they retreated.
On the 15th, the Germans penetrated the suburbs of Kerch.
ABOVE. Russian tanks, followed by infantry, advance through
enemy shell fire during a counter-attack in the Crimea.

DESERT WARFARE. After heavy dive bombing attacks on the British positions in Libya, General Rommel, on May 26, launched a full scale offensive aimed at defeating the British armored forces and capturing Tobruk. His plan of campaign called for the capture of Bir Hakeim, at the southern end of the British minefields, and the advance of the Afrika Korps, supported by German and Italian mobile divisions, round the southern end of the minefields. At the same time a holding attack was to be made on British positions running south from Gazala to the Trigh Capuzzo. On the night of May 26-27, Rommel carried out the first part of his plan. The Afrika Korps passed round Bir Hakeim and advanced rapidly towards El Duda and Sidi Rezegh. A few enemy tanks reached the escarpment overlooking the coastal road north of Acroma, before they were driven back. On the same night the enemy attempted a landing from the sea at this spot with the object of joining up with the tanks, but this move was frustrated by British naval units closely cooperating with the Army. Before the Axis forces reached El Adem and Acroma, they were drawn into action by British mechanized divisions and turned back. The attack on the British positions between Gazala and Trigh Capuzzo, made on the 27th, was repulsed, and the attack on Bir Hakeim by the Italian Mobile Corps was unsuccessful. The accompanying pictures, taken during the opening stages of the offensive, show: UPPER. Part of a German armored division advancing through a heavy artillery barrage. LOWER. Axis tanks being rushed up to the main battle area to reinforce their hard-pressed, retreating forces.

TOBRUK FALLS. After the withdrawal of the British forces to the Egyptian frontier, mobile formations harassed enemy columns pushing eastward toward Bardia and turned them back about twenty-five miles from the town. On June 20, 1942, however, Rommel's tank forces suddenly switched their attack towards Tobruk from the direction of El Adem and El Duda, and succeeded, with the help of massed dive bomber attacks, in forcing a gap on a narrow front in the southeast perimeter through which tanks and infantry passed. On the 21st, after desperate fighting, the town and port were occupied and the garrison of 25,000 was forced to surrender. On the same day the enemy occupied Bardia. By June 26, after capturing Capuzzo, Sollum, Helafaya, and Sidi Barrani, the enemy spearheaded within fifteen miles of Mersa Matruh, and on the next day he was joined by his main armored forces.

As a result Mersa Matruh fell and the British Eighth Army retreated rapidly towards El Alamein. Tanks of the Italian Littorio Division were pressed into an attack against the Eighth Army on June 30. The attack was repulsed and Italian losses were numerous. The following day Rommel hurled his infantry into battle against the South African division holding the north end of the line, and was met with a furious counter-attack. Only seventy miles now separated German troops from Alexandria, the key to the Suez Canal, and Cairo, the capital of Egypt. It was at this time that General Sir Harold Alexander, accompanied by General Bernard L. Montgomery, arrived upon the scene to subsequently save the situation. British gunners (above) pound the enemy with shells in a desperate effort to hold Mersa Matruh prior to their retreat to El Alamein.

GENERAL ROMMEL. In February 1941, after brilliant success in Europe, Lieutenant General Erwin Rommel was sent to Africa to head the Afrika Korps, following the rout of the Italians by the British. He began a counter-attack that covered 1,125 miles in two months and drove the British back to the Egyptian border. Early in 1942 he was made a Field Marshal and after a successful campaign Rommel was finally checked by General Sir Bernard L. Montgomery at El Alamein and driven out of Africa. This photograph of the Marshal was taken from a Nazi prisoner captured by Fifth Army forces in Italy. Rommel's record on the European continent and in Africa made him one of the outstanding generals of the war. Practically obscure before the start of hostilities in 1939, his first great success was scored during the conquest of France. It was the mechanized divisions under Rommel that breached the French line in the Sedan sector and made the famous drive towards the English Channel. This operation cut off the British and Belgians from the French Army and made the evacuation of Dunkirk imperative. After he was sent to Africa, Rommel's reputation grew at an even greater pace. During early 1942 he was practically unbeatable. One of his quirks was a habit of entertaining captured English officers. During these soirees he derived considerable pleasure from lecturing his prisoners on military tactics and pointing out to them the mistakes responsible for their downfall. In 1943, Rommel nearly accomplished the supreme objective of driving a wedge to the Suez Canal, a task which the Italians had embarked upon in 1940 with little success against the British.

BATTLE OF EGYPT. After the fall of Mersa Matruh, Rommel continued his advance eastwards, and by July 1, had succeeded in reaching El Alamein, only sixty miles from Alexandria. It was here that General Sir Claude Auchinleck decided to make a stand, for the country formed a narrow bottleneck, the sea guarding his right flank, and the Qattara Depression his left. In the early morning of July 1, the armored strength of the opposing forces joined battle, and heavy fighting ensued throughout the day. The Eighth Army repulsed repeated attacks by tanks and infantry, and on the evening of the 2nd the enemy retired, leaving the British positions intact. On the following day the British forces, with air support on a scale unprecedented on the Middle Eastern Front, counter-attacked, captured several hundred prisoners, and put numerous enemy tanks out of action. This was followed on July 10 by a co-ordinated attack by British and South African troops who, with tank and air support, managed to occupy the ridge of Tel el Eisa after a five mile advance. A similar attack was launched from the south on July 15 by New Zealand and

Indian infantry who succeeded in taking Ruweisat Ridge, south of El Alamein, and advancing into the enemy positions seven miles. UPPER LEFT. British tanks open an offensive at dawn on enemy strongpoints. UPPER RIGHT. Matildas, followed by men of the Scots Guards, cautiously advance in the vicinity of El Alamein. LOWER LEFT. A British soldier scans the horizon for signs of enemy troops while another stands ready for action at a Bren gun. LOWER RIGHT. Bren gun carrier narrowly escapes a mortar burst. One of the deciding factors in the battle for the control of Africa was the battle of logistics. Both the British and Germans were aware of the importance of keeping the supply lines open. Despite ceaseless attacks made by the R.A.F. and the British Navy, German supplies kept pouring into Africa through the port of Benghazi. The "Luftwaffe" hammered away at the longer and more difficult British line of supply. As the first Flying Fortresses, with General Lewis H. Brereton in command, were being rushed to give air support to the Eighth Army, supplies from America were slowly wending their way around the Cape of Good Hope,

FIGHTING IN THE DON BEND. Although the Germans had reached the gates of Voronezh, they were unable to take it by storm. Farther south, a rapid advance along the railways brought about the fall of Kantemirovka (south of Rossosh) and of Lisichansk (100 miles southwest of Kantemirovka) on July 12. Heavy fighting was in progress near Boguchar which, together with Millerovsk, the Russians were obliged to evacuate on the 15th. This created a dangerous bulge in the Russian lines which threatened the industrial city of Stalingrad, on the

Volga, and the port of Rostov at the mouth of the Don. The Russian armies inside the Don Bend fought fierce rearguard actions while they retired to their main defensive positions along the lower reaches of the river. However, by the 16th, fighting was taking place before Voroshilovgrad, and two days later the enemy, still advancing, was only seventy miles northwest of Rostov. On July 17, Voroshilovgrad was evacuated by the Red Army. LEFT. Russian sappers clear a way through a minefield. RIGHT. Soviet infantry firing automatic weapons.

RUSSIAN PORT EVACUATED. After the evacuation of Voroshilovgrad, the German attack on Rostov was broadened both
from Taganrog and Millerovo. On July 25, the enemy thrusts
down the railways from Voroshilovgrad and Millerovo linked
up, and fighting on the lower Don front became intensive. Two
bridges were thrown across the river at Tsymlyansk, and despite
desperate Russian resistance, the railway joining Stalingrad
with the Black Sea and the Caucasus was threatened. The enemy's superiority in arms and numbers enabled him to close in

on Rostov. After carrying out thorough demolitions, the great
port was evacuated by the Russians on the 27th. On the same
day another enemy threat to the Black Sea coast, and to the
oil of Maikop, took shape in a swift German drive southeast-
ward toward Bataisk. LEFT. German infantry crawl forward in
Rostov supported by field pieces. UPPER RIGHT. Burnt-out
street cars recently used as barricades by the Russians during
desperate street fighting which raged in the town and its suburbs. LOWER RIGHT. Germans surrender to Soviet tank crew.

RUSSIAN OIL FIELDS THREATENED. After the capture of Rostov and Bataisk, fighting took place near Salsk and Kuschev. Soviet forces were driven back and on August 6, von Kleist's tanks entered Tikhpretsk. The Germans continued their advance on Maikop, and on the 8th, broke through toward Armavir and Krasnodar. UPPER LEFT. Red troops attack an outpost. LOWER LEFT. German troops occupy a railway station. UPPER RIGHT. Germans advance along a choked road. LOWER RIGHT. Germans attack a strongpoint.

BOUND FOR FRANCE. On August 19, 1942, the Allies made a daring raid on the French coastal town of Dieppe. The knowledge gleaned from this attack, made under the direction of Admiral Mountbatten, enabled the Allies to assemble data for the invasion of the French coast in 1944. Canadians and landing craft (above) head for the cliffs of Dieppe.

WOUNDED EVACUATED. The Commandos participating in the raid counted heavily on the element of surprise. As a group of landing craft approached Berneval it was sighted by a German patrol ship which immediately sent out an alarm for help. Since it was too late for the attackers to withdraw the raid pressed forward. ABOVE. Wounded soldiers are brought aboard a British destroyer as the raid progressed. Although casualties were numerous, fast work by medical detachments saved hundreds of lives.

MISSION ACCOMPLISHED. Throughout the Dieppe raid an extensive air umbrella provided support for the ground offensive. All during the day aerial warfare developed on a scale not seen since the Battle of Britain. Despite the fact that Allied airmen were operating over enemy controlled territory they shot down ninety-one planes and probably damaged and destroyed twice that number. The Germans tried to create the impression that the raid had been a full scale attempt at invasion. This factor had been foreseen and forestalled by a

B.B.C. broadcast to the French people during the early stages of the operation. The French were told that no invasion was contemplated, and were urged to avoid all action that would compromise their safety. Canadians, who formed five-sixths of the attacking forces, suffered 3,350 casualties. UPPER LEFT. Two Churchill tanks and a burning landing craft line the shore. LOWER LEFT. A British tank whose tractor had been torn off. UPPER RIGHT. Airmen who participated in the operation. LOWER RIGHT. The Commandos return.

GERMANS ENTER THE SUBURBS. Repeated, desperate, German attempts to capture Stalingrad were thwarted by equally desperate Russian demolition tactics which permitted nothing of value to be yielded to the enemy. While troop-laden transports (above) near the battle area, German soldiers enter a suburb (upper right), and inspect the factory they have captured (lower right). They approach a damaged turbine.

BATTLE PANORAMA. One of the great epics of the war was the defense of Stalingrad which marked the turning point in the German struggle with Russia. The siege began in the early summer of 1942, lasted until February of 1943, and cost the German Army some 330,000 troops. The Russian attack designed to end the siege was launched in October. While the German forces clung desperately to their positions, Soviet forces threw a ring around them. This encirclement was slowly tightened until German troops were forced to depend on the arrival of supplies by air. As German planes flew in reinforcements, they were pounced upon by Russian fighters. Russian orders of surrender, directed to Colonel General Friedrich von Paulus, the Commander of the Sixth Army, were rejected, and on January 10, Russian units began the complete annihilation of German forces. By February 2 the fighting ceased, and the Russians reclaimed what was left of their former industrial center. UPPER. Russian soldiers fight amid the ruins. LOWER. Battle tested Soviet soldiers charge under fire.

THE INVASION OF NORTH AFRICA. Both to placate Russian demands for the opening of a second front, and to com-
ply with President Roosevelt's order directing the U.S. Chiefs
of Staff to stage an offensive European ground action (which

would offer encouragement to the peoples of the Allied nations and Axis-dominated countries), Operation "Torch" was
planned by the combined chiefs of staff of the U.S. and Great
Britain. ABOVE. The great armada as seen from escort carrier.

AMERICANS LAND IN FRENCH NORTH AFRICA.
Early on November 8, a few hours after parties of the
American Expeditionary Force had been put ashore at
many points on the coasts of Algeria and Morocco, the
world heard the news of the greatest combined military operation in history. The statement, issued from
Allied headquarters, revealed that the entire operation
was under the supreme command of Lieutenant-General
(now General of the Army) Dwight D. Eisenhower of the
United States Army, and was supported by powerful
units of the Royal Navy and Allied Air Forces. Steps
were taken to immediately inform the French people,
by radio and leaflets, of the landings and to assure
them that the Allies sought no territory and had no
intention of interfering with the French authorities in
Africa. The landings were designed to forestall the occupation by the Axis powers of any part of North or
West Africa, and to deny the enemy a starting point
from which a possible attack might be launched against
the Atlantic seaboards of the American and the British
West Indies. They also provided an effective second
front for relieving pressure on the Russians and, moreover, comprised the first bold step toward the liberation of France and her Empire. Another important factor was the timing of the landings which coincided with
the British Eighth Army's offensive against Rommel in
the Western desert. The outstanding initial success of
the operation was due, not only to the perfect cooperation among the Allied forces, but also to the great
secrecy which had been maintained throughout. Winston
Churchill, in a speech before the House of Commons on
November 11, revealed that orders for the expedition
to French North Africa had been issued as early as
July, 1942, for a vast convoy of ships had to be assembled to carry the tens of thousands of troops and their
equipment to the landing beaches. This armada included
more than 500 transports with about 350 protecting naval
vessels. Powerful air cover was provided for the convoy
all the time it was at sea. Despite the great hazards of
the route across the Atlantic and through the Western
Mediterranean, all the ships arrived safely. The troops
disembarked under cover of darkness and were con-
voyed from the transports to the beaches in auxiliary
landing craft. The picture (right) shows but a small
part of the huge convoy which assured the victory.

THE INVASION OF
NORTH AFRICA

By Admiral H. K. Hewitt, USN

THE INVASION of North Africa, the beginning of the drive to make contact with Axis forces on continental Europe, was decided upon in July, 1942. The Allies hoped for light opposition, or none at all, from the French.

There were three main objectives in the Allied plans. Casablanca, on the coast of French Morocco, was to be taken by United States Army and Naval forces, while a Naval force, primarily British, was to land U.S. Army and British Army forces for the seizure of Algiers and Oran on the coast of Algeria. D-Day was to be November 8.

The U.S. Navy, except for one division of transports and other small units in the Algerian operation, saw most of its action in connection with the taking of Casablanca. The plans called for three landings, so that troops could close in on Casablanca itself from north and south, and so that the large airfield near Port Lyautey could be seized and utilized. The main landing was to be at Fedala, 14 miles north of Casablanca, just beyond range of the fixed defenses of that city. The secondary landings were at the mouth of the Sebou River, near Port Lyautey, 65 miles to the northward, and at Safi, a small port 190 miles to the southward. The capture of the latter port, with its docks, was essential to the prompt landing of tanks from the ships which carried them. (Special tank landing ships had not then become available.) The infantry division from Fedala was to advance south, and the armored force from Safi north, for the investment of Casablanca.

The large convoy of transports, supply ships, supporting battleships, cruisers, carriers and escorting destroyers sailed from ports in the U.S. (principally Hampton Roads), and Bermuda, effected rendezvous at sea, and proceeded by devious routes across the Atlantic, without loss from submarine attack. Radio silence was maintained throughout. At daylight of November 7, estimate of coastal surf conditions being favorable, the decision was made to land on the scheduled date, and the various task forces separated to take their assigned stations.

ZERO HOUR

THE ZERO hour for the landings was about three hours before daylight. All were made satisfactorily and very close to schedule. At Safi, where there was no beach outside the breakwater, two old world war destroyers, the "Cole" and the "Bernadou," with masts cut down to give a low silhouette, loaded with specially trained assault troops, dashed inside the harbor and alongside the dock or breakwater, catching the defenses completely by surprise. At the River Sebou, a similar destroyer, the "Dallas," rammed the harbor defense net and, ultimately, with the aid of a Port Lyautey pilot (who had been secretly brought to the U.S. for the purpose), proceeded up river to a point off the air field.

The French, unfortunately, resisted at all points, and it was necessary to return their fire. The shore batteries at Fedala were quickly silenced by the fire of the supporting cruisers, "Augusta" and "Brooklyn," and by the pugnacious U.S. destroyers which went in to close range.

The French light forces in Casablanca, under cover of smoke screens, made repeated gallant efforts to attack the transports off Fedala. They were driven off, and eventually all were destroyed or severely damaged by gunfire, or air attack, or by a combination of the two. The immobile, partially completed "Jean Bart," whose one quadruple 15" turret was used as part of the Casablanca defenses, was hit by 16" shells from the "Massachusetts," and by air bombs. She was damaged and sunk at her dock, but her turret remained in action.

At 7:55 a.m., November 11th, five minutes before the opening of the final assault on Casablanca by combined sea, naval, air, and ground forces, word of an armistice was received, and hostile operations ceased.

On the nights of November 11th and November 12th, before they could be brought in to the wrecked harbor of Casablanca, four transports, engaged in unloading important supplies for the troops ashore, were torpedoed and sunk in the transport area off Fedala. A tanker, a supply ship, and a destroyer were also damaged by the assembling German submarines.

The U.S. Navy set up sea frontier forces (surface and air) based on Casablanca and the air station at Port Lyautey for the protection of convoys and allied shipping in the approaches to Casablanca and the western and southwestern approaches to the Straits of Gibraltar. The U.S. Navy also set up an operating base for the control of the port of Oran. Both of these activities subsequently became part of the "U.S. Naval Forces North West African Waters" when that command was established, in February 1943, with headquarters in Algiers.

H. K. Hewitt

THE INVASION BEGINS. On November 7, ships from the convoy steamed past Gibraltar, the headquarters of the operation. General Giraud, the choice of Londoners and Washingtonians to head the French forces in Africa, flew to Gibraltar to confer with General Eisenhower. The interview proved to be a stormy one. General Giraud assumed that he was to be placed in supreme command of the expedition and at first refused to serve in any other capacity. He later modified his demands and agreed to take charge of all French forces in North Africa which would rally to the side of the Allies. During the early morning hours of November 8, the first news of the operation materialized. Initial reports revealed that the landing at Algiers had met with little opposition. ABOVE. The picture shows an anti-aircraft barrage put up against enemy night bombers in the harbor of Algiers. Enemy air activity was especially heavy in this sector. The intensity of the fire from guns aboard the transports and combat ships in this area alone accounted for 83 German planes during November 8-20, 1942. Six months after the landings the last German soldier in Africa surrendered.

FRENCH RESISTANCE. At first the French resisted the British-American landings in North Africa. The French fleet, especially, put up a stout fight. But they soon saw the light. General Charles de Gaulle, head of the Fighting French, and General Henri Giraud, High Commissioner in North Africa, "got together" and joined in the battle to drive the Axis powers from Africa. UPPER. First U.S. flag goes up on a beachhead at Fedala Harbor, French Morocco, November 9, 1942. LOWER. Troops stand guard over a captured French train and crew at St. Leu, Algeria, on November 8.

FIREFIGHTING ABOARD A CARRIER. The most modern scientific equipment, and men specially trained in the Navy's fire-fighter schools are ready for crash landings aboard a carrier. UPPER. An F4U flames wildly after crash landing aboard an "Essex"-class carrier. Shot up by enemy action, the plane landed out of control and was cut in two just aft of the cockpit. Within second fire fighters are on the scene, the crew has been rescued, and foamite is sprayed on the fire. LOWER. The fire is brought under control. Various agents are used to extinguish fires depending on the material involved. Foamite smothers burning gasoline very rapidly.

DISASTER AT ALGIERS. A spectacular photograph, but one which illustrates the fact that all our losses were not due to enemy action. Here two Liberty ships which had brought supplies to support our activities in the Mediterranean, burn at Algiers on 16 July 1943. The USS "Savannah" is in the foreground. It is only in rare cases that the trained men of the crews cannot cope with fire aboard ship with a minimum of damage to the equipment and cargo.

D-DAY AT ORAN. United States forces met with bitter resistance, especially from French naval elements. The famous
U.S. 1st Division (whose name became synonymous with offensive action throughout the war), supported by the 1st
Armored Division, was soon able to submit favorable battle
reports. General Terry de la M. Allen, who later commanded
the 104th Division in Europe, and General Fredendall acquitted their first battle tests admirably. French resistance against
British and American troops ceased three days after the
landings. ABOVE. Coming ashore near Oran on D-Day. The
landings in Africa surprised the Axis who had anticipated an
invasion of the European continent.

ALLIED AIR SUPREMACY. The British Eighth Army, commanded by General Montgomery, began to assault German positions at El Alamein on October 23, 1942. Within two weeks the Germans were retreating westward. In mid-November General Anderson, Commander of the British First Army, advanced towards Tunis and Bizerte, and by December 1, there was bitter fighting in Tunisia centered around Mateur and Djedeida. On December 13, Rommel's armies were routed at El Agheila. The R.A.F. delivered incessant day and night attacks on the fast retreating enemy. Lines of enemy vehicles were wrecked, ammunition dumps were blown up, and enemy airfields were strafed. LEFT. The twisted remains of an airfield near Libya. RIGHT. Bullet-riddled Italian fighters.

AMERICAN EAGLES. ABOVE. American B-25 bombers fly over their base after taking off on a bombing mission. Bombers like these, and C-47's (the "flying boxcars" of the Air Transport Command which rushed supplies to the front), played an important role in the defeat of the Axis in Tunisia. One of Rommel's greatest advantages at this time was the possession of all-weather airstrips, as the development of the rainy season rendered fighter-plane support of the Allied troops impossible. The easily maintained air and sea lanes of Axis communications permitted a rapid build-up of supplies.

FRENCH COMMANDER SHOT. On December 24, 1942, Admiral Jean Francois Darlan, self-appointed High Commissioner of French North and West Africa (who had been backed as a "temporary expedient" by the U.S. Government), was shot to death in Algiers. The assassin, 20-year-old Bonnier de la Chapelle, member of a French patriotic youth organization which aided Allied landings in North Africa, was tried by court martial and executed two days later. The Admiral's death precipitated a political crisis which resulted in the French North African Government's designation of Gen. Henri Giraud as Commander of the French troops. Admiral Darlan (above) is shown with General Eisenhower.

NEW RED OFFENSIVE. On Christmas Day, 1942, the Russian
Army launched a new thrust against the enemy southeast of
Nalchik and recaptured Alagir and Krasnogorsk, thereby re-
gaining the use of the Ossetian military highway. On December 26, Soviet ski troops advanced thirty miles across the
snow and wiped out a Nazi salient which still menaced the
Grozny oilfields. On January 3, 1943, Mozdok, the important
communications center of the Caucasus, was retaken in a

surprise attack by Cossack Guards. With Mozdok in Russian hands, access to the Grozny oilfields was denied to the invader. ABOVE. A column of Russian ski troops clad in white uniforms advances over the snow. Troops such as these played an important role in the Red Army's winter offensive. The white uniforms of the Soviet soldiers provided en effective means of camouflage by enabling them to "disappear" at will into the snow covered countryside.

DESERT WARFARE. Continuing through Tripolitania, the British Eighth Army chased the dwindling Afrika Korps along the coast road. The retreating enemy columns suffered continuous bombing from the air by the powerful Western Desert air force. On December 25, 1942, British troops occupied Sirte without opposition, but to the west of this town air operations were curtailed because of violent sandstorms. Beyond the Wadi Bei-el-Kebir, the Eighth Army's sappers were busily engaged for several days clearing away mines and booby traps which the Germans had strewn over the roads in great numbers in order to delay the advance. On January 5, 1943, Allied forces entered Buerat-el Hsun, about sixty miles west of Sirte where the coast road turns north along the salt marshes towards Misurata and Tripoli. After crossing the Wadi Zemzem on January 14, the Eighth Army troops encountered enemy rearguards at a point 70 miles from Misurata, but Rommel soon abandoned all his defensive positions in the area. Four days later Misurata was occupied without any opposition. By January 20, the Eighth Army had progressed along the coast beyond Misurata to the important defensive positions of Homs and Tahuna, and on the following day advanced British columns had entered the suburbs of Tripoli, whose capture was announced less than 48 hours afterwards. Meanwhile heavy day and night blows were delivered against Tripoli harbor and the great Axis airfield at Castel Benito on the outskirts of the city. The picture (left) shows British infantry advancing behind tanks in Tripolitania.

TWO SHOTS FROM BEHIND. This picture, found on a German officer as he was taken prisoner, bore no descriptive note, and needs none. It is eloquent of Nazi ruthlessness.

ALLIED CONFERENCE IN FRENCH MOROCCO. On January 14, the President of the United States and the Prime Minister of Great Britain met at Casablanca. A review of future Allied operations in the war was the purpose of the meeting. The leaders were accompanied by the combined Chiefs of Staff of the two countries and their expert advisers. This was the fourth meeting between Roosevelt and Churchill. The far-reaching importance of this conference in North Africa may be judged by the fact that it was the greatest gathering of Allied war chiefs convened since the outbreak of the second World War. Mr. Churchill left Britain on January 12 in the same Liberator which took him on his 1,000-mile trip to the Middle East and Moscow in August, 1942. President Roosevelt arrived in North Africa on January 14 after making the 5,000-mile flight across the Atlantic by Clipper. During the conference, which lasted ten days, the whole field of the second World War was surveyed in detail and all Allied resources were marshalled for the more intense prosecution of the war by land, air and sea. President Roosevelt, Mr. Churchill and their respective staffs arrived at complete agreement regarding plans for offensive operations which were to be undertaken by the Allies against the Axis in the 1943 campaigns. The conference also provided an opportunity for a meeting between the French leaders, Generals de Gaulle (right) and Giraud. This picture (above) depicts the historic meeting.

BRITISH ENTER TRIPOLI. At 5 A.M. on January 23, 1943, the victorious British Eighth Army entered Tripoli and the Union Jack was hoisted from a fort overlooking the harbor. Thus the last remaining capital of Mussolini's former empire passed into British hands, three months to the day since the offensive began at El Alamein. The final advance on the city came from three directions. Two columns of armored units and New Zealand infantry pushed through the desert to the south, while the British infantry advanced from the east along the coast road. Most of the inhabitants of the city lined the streets as columns of British tanks, armored vehicles and infantry filed into the main square from the suburbs. At noon, General Montgomery received the official surrender of Tripoli from the Vice-Governor of Libya at a point just outside the city walls. Since the attack at El Alamein the Eighth Army had advanced 1,400 miles in ninety days to reach Tripoli, an average of nearly sixteen miles a day. The photograph (above) catches enthusiastic Highlanders hoisting the Union Jack.

8TH ARMY OUSTS AXIS IN LIBYA. Advancing still west-
wards from Tripoli the Eighth Army maintained contact with
enemy rearguards, and on January 31 occupied the port of
Zuara, the last Italian town on the Tripolitanian coast. Meanwhile, advanced British patrols had already crossed the frontier into Tunisia to the south of the coastal road. On February
2, a 15-mile advance was made from Zuara to the village of
Zelten, beyond which artillery duels were exchanged with the
Axis forces withdrawing towards Pisada, only 12 miles from
the Tunisian frontier. For the next two weeks progress was
slower and operations on land were reduced to patrol activity. Then, on February 15, the Eighth Army occupied Ben
Gardane and its large airfield, and began the advance
towards Medenine and the Mareth Line. The photographs
depict: UPPER. A British anti-tank gun in action. LOWER.
British infantry under cover of a damaged German tank.

U.S. TROOPS FALL BACK IN TUNISIA. On February 14, while the Eighth Army was pushing forward to Medenine after capturing Ben Gardane, the Germans launched a strong attack against the relatively lightly held American lines in the central part of Tunisia. The attack was delivered by a German armored division in two columns. Supported by masses of fighter planes and dive bombers, the Germans quickly overran the advanced American positions and completely isolated some artillery and infantry units. Counter-attacks somewhat delayed the enemy's advance, but Axis reinforcements were brought up in very strong force with the result that the U.S. troops were compelled to evacuate the Gafsa Oasis and three of their forward airfields. ABOVE. A well-camouflaged British gun in action. UPPER LEFT. An American-built Priest gun-howitzer. LOWER LEFT. Allied troops under fire.

KASSERINE OFFENSIVE. The last Nazi offensive in Africa came at Kasserine Pass. It was launched by the veteran 21st Panzer Division on February 14, 1943. In very fierce fighting nearly half the tanks of our 1st Armored Division were lost. But reinforcements were sent in, and Rommel was driven back through this Pass. UPPER LEFT. Battery B, of the 33rd Field Artillery, set up a 105mm howitzer for defense at Kasserine. LOWER LEFT. The First Ranger Battalion on a speed march near Arzew, Algeria, during North African operation. ABOVE. Elements of the 2nd Battalion, 16th Infantry, march over a mine-cleared road, through Kasserine Pass, en route to Farriana, Tunisia.

BATTLE OF THE TANKS. In the Tunisian campaign the armored divisions of both sides counted greatly as strategic devices. Tank support was particularly indispensable to fully exploit breaks in the lines of the opposing forces. On March 6, 1943, the Germans made a concentrated assault on British positions in Southern Tunisia with infantry and tanks. It failed. The Nazis were forced to retreat to the hills north of Medenine, and in one day's fighting, 33 Axis tanks were destroyed without the loss of a single British tank. Two days later enemy tanks captured by the British totaled 50. At the end of February, the important Kasserine Pass, a fiercely contested objective when taken from the Allies a week earlier, was successfully regained and cleared of the enemy. The end was in sight for the Germans in Tunisia as British forces seized the heights overlooking the coastal road to Tunis under heavy fighting and penetrated enemy positions. On all fronts the Allied armies continued to beat back the Axis lines, with war maps showing eight separate actions as Rommel's armies retreated to the Gulf of Tunis. American and British infantry supported by tanks forced the withdrawal. The Germans retreated with such speed after repeated pounding by American artillery that they abandoned their unburied dead. Thus it was necessary for Allied troops to bury those whom they had killed in the battle. Synchronizing the campaign in Tunis, General Eisenhower sent 100 Flying Fortresses into Naples, Italy, causing major losses to enemy positions there, while in Africa for a distance of 100 miles the flames could be seen streaking skyward over Rommel's air bases of supply. To further help solidify the hold of the Allies in the Mediterranean theatre of war, General Doolittle's U.S. Eighth Air Force went after the Italian Navy, smashing two heavy cruisers off Sardinia. Among the prisoners of war in Africa were many Italians. As the Eighth Army advanced and the number of enemy prisoners increased, the ratio of captured Italians to Germans was, on many occasions, found to be six to one, showing that the Germans had no conscience in deserting the soldiers of Italy, then their ally. The accompanying pictures show some of the incidents during this stage of fighting in Tunisia. UPPER. British tank crews mounting before an advance against enemy positions. LOWER. Hundreds of war-weary Italian soldiers, a thoroughly disaffected lot, surrender in a latter stage of the campaign.

EIGHTH ARMY STRIKES NORTH AGAIN. After capturing the port of Sfax on April 10, 1943, the Eighth Army pushed northward over terrain which had been heavily mined. In spite of these obstacles the advance was rapid over the 80-mile stretch to Sousse—taken by the Allies on April 12 without opposition. However, the enemy had destroyed the port, dock installations, and utilities before evacuating. While Rommel's armies suffered heavy casualties during their retreat from the Mareth Line, the bulk of the Afrika Korps escaped to Enfidaville. Since March 20, the British Eighth Army alone had taken 20,000 prisoners in Tunisia. LEFT. Sappers of the Eighth Army repair a bridge over the river at Gabes. RIGHT. General Montgomery triumphantly enters the port of Sousse.

VICTORY IN TUNISIA. By date of the Casablanca Conference it had become apparent that our adventure in North Africa was to be successful, even beyond hopes and expectations. As General Marshall said, "Tunisia was a lure into which the German command continued to pour great quantities of men and materiel, commitments that were certain to be disastrous for the enemy . . ." At the conclusion of the North African campaign with the mass surrender of Axis forces in Tunisia, enemy killed and captured numbered 349,206, and 200,000 tons of German and Italian materiel had been captured or destroyed on land alone. UPPER LEFT. Members of Battery G, 209th Coast Artillery, firing a 40mm Bofors antiaircraft gun at Berteaux, Algeria. LOWER LEFT. Night fighters of a rifle brigade of the First Armored Division holding position in a wrecked building in Tunisia on April 5, 1943. Picture was made a month before Axis forces in Tunisia were cut in two, and the battle was raging at this time. UPPER RIGHT. This is a crossroads extending to Mateur and Tunis. Battle was soon to reach the showdown stage. Here, on May 3, 1943, a tank heads for Mateur. LOWER RIGHT. A battalion of the 60th Infantry advances up a hill about 10 miles from Bizerte. This picture was made about 2:30 P.M. on May 7, 1943, shortly before American troops entered that city. In many respects, the fighting in Tunisia taught the American GI and his officers many of the lessons of war. It was a hard schoolroom, but it had the effect of making tough veterans out of green and hitherto untried soldiers.

PATTERN OF WAR. The Nazis tried to drive us out of our North African strongholds with every means at hand. Air raids were frequent, but they were invariably met with ack-ack fire like that (above) going up during a raid on Algiers. UPPER RIGHT. Shortly after this picture was made on May 6, 1943, these American troops helped to take Mateur. LOWER RIGHT. American infantrymen are warily searching Bizerte for snipers. After the fall of Bizerte and Tunis, they were used as springboards—along with many other African bases—for the Sicilian and Salerno landings. Real property in Tunisia took a beating during our campaign there. Bizerte, particularly, was almost ruined.

IN PREPARATION TO STORM BEACHHEADS. Lined up
along the docks of a North African port, a flotilla of LST's
(landing ship-tanks) take on board a great number of sup-

plies, vehicles, and men preparatory to invasion on enemy
shores. The LST's played a prominent part in the invasion of
North Africa and proved indispensable in later invasions.

EIGHTH ARMY WELCOMES ROYALTY. On June 12 a service plane with two wing commanders at the controls landed on a North African airfield. Luggage in the plane was labelled T. Jerram, but out stepped King George VI to be welcomed by General Eisenhower, Admiral Cunningham, and Air Chief Marshal Tedder. The King had borrowed the name of Guardsman Jerram, his orderly, for his visit to the Eighth Army—the first time a King of England had ever flown to a battlefront. For several days he busied himself with consultations with service commanders, visits to the men of the forces, who welcomed him warmly, meetings with American military and naval leaders, and other activities. He spent a day with the Navy, shaking hands with many of the men who had seen action at Pantelleria, and talking to merchant sailors engaged in hazardous convoy duty. With Sir Andrew Cunningham, he visited units of the U.S. and British fleets, being piped aboard a British battleship and an American cruiser. The King inspected American infantry, watched a parade of armored forces, and exercises in street fighting. He invited Generals Giraud and de Gaulle to lunch along with Robert Murphy, the American minister, and the British resident minister, Harold Macmillan. One of his visits, unofficial and unexpected, gave rise to a remarkable display of loyalty and enthusiasm. At a big convalescent rest center by the sea, where several thousand soldiers were recuperating from wounds and illness, word flashed round that the King had arrived. Swiftly men raced to greet him— crowding, laughing, and cheering wildly. Many of them dashed out of the water to be among the first to shake their visitor's hand. Somebody started to sing the National Anthem. It was taken up with fervor, and when it was finished the men cheered the King enthusiastically. In the accompanying picture the King walks between packed lines of soldiers on the sand dunes of Africa.

NAVAL PATROL BOMBER SCORES A HIT. Flying in a U.S.
Navy plane a Navy photographer snapped this remarkable
close-up of a direct hit on a surfaced German U-Boat. One

bare-legged crewman stands in awe of the column of spray
as another ducks. A second depth charge has been dropped
(arrow) in an attempt to finish off the undersea raider.

THE UNITED STATES NAVY IN
THE INVASION OF SICILY

By Vice Admiral Richard L. Conolly, USN

BY MID-MAY of 1943, the Germans and Italians had surrendered in North Africa, and our military forces in that area were powerful enough to justify planning a major offensive operation against "Festung Europa," the fortress Europe.

Unique features of this operation were that it was to be mounted largely in North Africa from ports extending from Oran to Alexandria, and it was to employ in addition to the usual large transports with their embarked landing craft, a host of newly constructed landing ships, intermediate sized self-sustaining landing craft and support craft. All this armada had to be assembled in small North African ports, trained, organized, and rehearsed with the troop units to be landed.

The whole tremendous operation, air, naval, and ground force, was planned under the aegis of Allied Force Headquarters. The combined naval force with embarked troops was commanded by Admiral Sir Andrew Browne Cunningham, the Commander-in-Chief, Mediterranean, a British flag officer of pre-eminent record and vast experience in those waters. It was divided into Eastern and Western Naval Task Forces, commanded respectively by a British and an American vice admiral. Each of these major subdivisions was further divided into three subordinate task forces, each in turn commanded by a rear admiral. Included in the general plan were vast air forces and powerful naval covering forces, the latter for protection against the beaten, but still potentially dangerous Italian Fleet.

THE LANDINGS

ALL THE many naval components took a preliminary staging disposition and later departed from staging ports on a vast and intricate schedule. The seamanship of the newly organized naval forces was tested severely by the rough weather encountered en route. However, the attack was delivered simultaneously and the troops were landed successfully and with complete tactical surprise during darkness of the early morning of 10 July 1943. Major landing forces were put ashore at five principal positions. Three of these objectives, Scoglitti, Gela, and Licata, on the south coast of Sicily, were attacked by the American task force (Western).

The landing at Scoglitti, preceded by bombardment by our naval units, was accomplished with comparatively little opposition, the Italian troops abandoning their defense positions during the pre-invasion bombardment.

At Gela the troops landed exactly on schedule, and the first waves encountered slight opposition. The second wave met stiff resistance and suffered heavy casualties until shore batteries were silenced by the naval gunfire from the U.S. cruisers "Savannah" and "Boise."

At Licata the larger part of the assault infantry were transported to anchorages off the landing beaches in thirty-six new LST's which had been converted by the installation of six landing craft, each of which landed an assault platoon. Heavy opposition was encountered on the left flank, but all beaches were captured and the unloading of supplies began.

After the landings, the participating naval forces were subjected to intense enemy air attack for three days. The enemy also launched violent counter-attacks on our troops, spearheaded with tanks which threatened to drive our forces near Gela into the sea. Accurate naval gunfire broke up these attacks and served as antitank fire for the men on the beaches. Had there been no naval support, these attacks might have succeeded in destroying our forces in that area.

SUPPORTING FORCES

AS THE combined troops drove ahead from the landing beaches they were supported, whenever possible, by our naval forces. At Porto Empedocle and Agrigento this support contributed greatly to the capture of those positions. The resistance met by our ground troops consisted mainly of small arms fire, since almost every large gun was spotted and destroyed by well directed naval fire.

Destroyers and small craft took a major part in the protection of transports against the almost continuous German air attacks. These small craft also protected captured harbors, swept enemy mines, performed necessary salvage, and opened up ports essential for the support of the Seventh Army.

This operation was a triumph of planning and an example of what can be accomplished by a generous spirit between the Army and Naval Forces and between two allies, all working enthusiastically toward the same end on approved plans. The Invasion of Sicily was the prototype of large-scale amphibious landings that were to prove so irresistibly effective throughout the ensuing campaigns of the war.

R L Conolly

GI JOE. Despite all the scientific and technological advances of warfare, that familiar character, GI Joe, with his feet on the ground and in the mud, marked our progress along the road to victory in World War II. It was he who actually came to grips with the enemy. ABOVE. A mortar squad of these Joes going about the business of war in the ruins of St. Malo, France. Men like these knew most of war's casualties.

THE BREAKOUT. After invasion and establishment of a beachhead on Normandy the first big Allied drive came with the breakout at St. Lo. The ring that had held us near the sea was burst open on July 25 after an unprecedented saturation bombing by Allied air forces. Troops swept inland then with fierce fighting, encircled the German Seventh Army and virtually annihilated it by August 19. ABOVE. Two youngsters view the ruins of St. Lo.

OPERATION HUSKY. After the brilliant success of the Tunisian campaign, plans were made for toppling Mussolini and eliminating Italy from the war. After two months of preparation these plans went into effect. They were called Operation Husky—the invasion of Sicily. On the early morning of July 10, 1943, some 160,000 Allied troops in more than 3,000 vessels struck this Italian island. Troops involved were the British Eighth and the American Seventh Armies. The latter was commanded by General George S. Patton, Jr., and included the 1st, 3rd, 9th and 42nd Infantry Divisions, the 2nd Armored Division, and the 82nd Airborne Division. Under cover of Naval artillery U.S. troops hit the beach at three points—Licata, Gela, and Scoglitti. The British landed from Cape Passero to Syracuse. UPPER. Assault troops boarding Higgins boats in a North African port, getting ready for the strike. LOWER. The American light cruiser "Boise," sailing across the bow of LST 325, hurls shells on enemy positions on the southern coast near Gela on August 11. Despite such bombardment, opposition was stiff at some points when troops hit the beaches.

FROM AFRICA TO SICILY. After the Tunisian campaign ended and the Axis armies had been driven out of the African continent, the victorious Allies were soon in a position to make their next move in the Mediterranean war zone. The capture of the small, but strategically important, island of Pantelleria gave the British and U.S. air forces valuable advanced airfields to complement those at Malta and along the North African shores. For any amphibious military operations against the Mediterranean coastline of Europe powerful support by fighter cover, or "air umbrella," was absolutely necessary. Indeed, as experience in this war had already shown, no landings on an enemy-occupied coast, however skilfully planned and boldly executed, could hope to be successful without such fighter cover. The map (right), shows the approximate operational range of fighter aircraft based along the southern shores of the Mediterranean, including the islands of Malta and Pantelleria. It reveals quite clearly, therefore, why Sicily (although it was known to be the most strongly defended of all the chief Italian islands) was selected for the initial attack on the "under belly" of Europe, instead of Sardinia or Corsica. As the map shows, Sicily lay well within operational range of Allied fighter aircraft, whereas Sardinia was only partly within their range, and Corsica right outside it. It follows, therefore, that while fighters could have accompanied military landings on Sardinia, they could not have covered such landings in anything approaching sufficient strength. Over Sicily, on the other hand, strong fighter protection could be provided quite easily. Another important factor which the Allied commanders must have undoubtedly had in mind when the decision to attack Sicily was made was its possession of a large number of first-class airfields which would prove of the greatest value for the next step in the Mediterranean campaign, the attack on the Italian mainland.

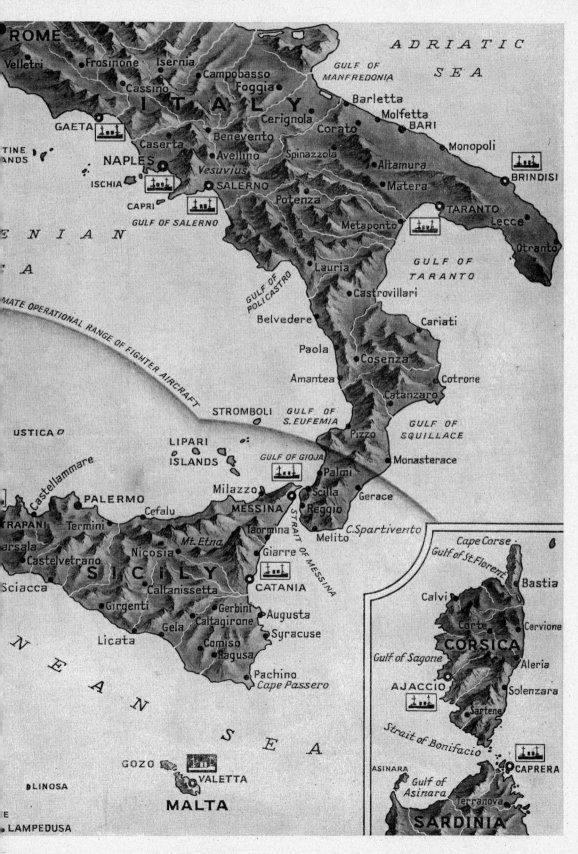

THE GERMANS STRIKE. The German air force opposed our landings in Sicily vigorously during initial stages of the assault, but was soon driven away. UPPER. Ships of the invasion fleet, whose numbers burdened the Mediterranean, send up a terrific barrage of flak as enemy bombers come in on July 10 and drop flares to see what's going on below. The bombers came in during daylight the next day (lower). This action took place off Gela. The ship in background at far left came near being hit by the bomb exploding in the water. Actually, little damage was done.

IT TAKES EVERYTHING. UPPER. Army mules—Mediter-ranean type—come ashore at Licata with the greatest reluct-ance. These beasts of burden, though ornery, were invaluable in our advance over the rough Sicilian terrain. For some reason, Mussolini had not troubled to add to the few roads on this outpost to Italy. LOWER. Paratroops advancing through the Sicilian countryside on July 11 after landing the night before. These airborne ground troops played a signifi-cant role in our acquisition of Sicily. Later, they came to the aid of hard-pressed U.S. troops in the Salerno invasion.

COLORFUL PATTON. One of the most colorful of World War II's generals was George S. Patton, Jr.—"Old Blood and Guts" to the men who followed him, and a terror to the Germans he opposed. UPPER LEFT. General Patton looks the situation over near the beach at Gela on July 11, shortly after that town fell to his forces. LOWER LEFT. On the same day the General (in second story window on right) takes a look at Italian prisoners in Gela. UPPER RIGHT. Italian tank blown up by American guns is shown in this Gela street scene July 11. A sign on the building above the smashed tank once read: "Mussolini's — Do Not Touch." Obviously, the American GI's didn't believe in signs. LOWER RIGHT. U.S. armored troops moving through Palma, Sicily, the day after the invasion. Under constant pounding from Allied ground troops, heavy bombing by our planes, and landings in the German rear, the enemy was forced to retire toward Messina. Seeing their situation was hopeless the Germans raced to Messina to escape across the narrow four-mile strait. Their air power and intense fire from coastal batteries enabled some 88,000 of them to get across in boats and barges, but they left much materiel.

THE HIGH PRICE OF WAR. UPPER. This is not a pleasant picture, but it indicates something of the price we paid for Sicily. These men are Americans—paratroopers slain near Vittoria, Sicily, July 13, 1943. They were killed by the most famous German gun—the 88—and by weapons of heavy tanks. The valor of such men as these brought our victory—not only on Sicily—but all over the world. LOWER. American troops are moving through a Sicilian street. Under General Patton's guidance, our 2nd Armored and 3rd Infantry Divisions moved up 72 miles in two days.

ITALIANS GIVE UP. UPPER. Shortly after the Allied assault on Sicily it was apparent that the Italians—who had been told by Mussolini to enjoy "living dangerously"—had little stomach for this fight. When the showdown between fight and surrender arrived, they usually chose to surrender. Many of them wanted to get on American ships in the harbor on the chance they they could get to the U.S. UPPER. Prisoners of the 3rd Infantry Division, taken in Agrigento. LOWER. A large rifle (6.1 inch) of the 36th Field Artillery ready to be moved up to the front.

ITALIAN DILEMMA. When American troops overran Sicily the bewildered Italians there didn't know whether to cheer or to glare. So most of them did both, alternately. Sometimes they cheered without reservation, sometimes they were openly hostile. ABOVE. This is a cheering section of citizens as U.S. troops enter Prizzi on August 20. UPPER RIGHT. The natives appear to have taken cover while our troops enter Palermo, one of the larger cities, on August 21. LOWER RIGHT. GIs of Company K, 15th Infantry, swing along a street in Palermo, August 23. For the most part, American soldiers were a hit with Sicilians, particularly the children, who discovered the Yanks' generosity.

THE ENEMY RETREATS. Before the assault of Allied forces, the Germans fell back, dynamiting bridges and mining roads. UPPER LEFT. This is the condition in which they left the bridges. This one, pictured on August 2, was between Mistretta and St. Stefano. Our motorized equipment is delayed, but infantry troops proceed on foot. LOWER LEFT. Retreat for great numbers of the enemy was cut off by American and British troops. This is a group of Germans and Italians captured when the 3rd Division made a surprise landing behind enemy lines and cut them off from their units near the town of Acquedolei on August 9. American troops shown are of the 30th Infantry Regiment of the 3rd Division. UPPER RIGHT. This is one of the well-known pictures of the war. Wounded by shrapnel shortly before the picture was made, August 9, a member of the 7th Infantry Regiment of the 3rd Division, is receiving blood plasma. LOWER RIGHT. A smokescreen demonstration at Palermo harbor, supervised by the Chemical officer of the 7th Army, on August 16. Smoke was used extensively for covering operations in nearly all theaters of the war.

SICILY CONQUERED. After the fall of Catania on August 5, 1943, British and Canadian forces pressed forward and made important gains north of Regalbuto. The British Eighth Army pressed northward along the coast road to Messina, 50 miles away. Ships of the Allied fleets kept up a heavy bombardment of Messina. The Germans made every effort to delay the advance of the Allies by mines and large scale demolitions, but numbers of Germans and Italians were already assembling on the beaches of Messina preparatory to evacuation, and evacuation barges were being pounded and sunk by Allied planes. The Allies remained master of the air. According to R.A.F. statistics, 12,000 German and Italian aircraft had been destroyed in the Middle East and North African campaigns since the entry of Italy into the war. In Sicily alone, up to the surrender of Catania, the number of Axis prisoners totalled 100,000. On August 10 the Eighth Army and the U.S. Seventh Army linked up between Troina and Randazzo, and on the 17th the honor of capturing Messina fell to the Americans. All organized resistance on the island ceased. After a campaign of 39 days the Sicilian operation ended. Up to August 10 Axis losses were 167,000—32,000 killed or wounded, and 135,000 prisoners. Allied casualties totalled 25,000 killed, wounded, or taken prisoner. RIGHT. American troops move into Messina on August 17.

THE VICTORY CAKE. Victory in Sicily was sweet, and for General Patton a special victory cake was baked. UPPER. The General is putting the knife to it in September, 1943, after his victorious Seventh Army and the British had conquered the enemy. At left is Major General Geoffrey Keyes, Deputy Commander of the Seventh Army. Colonel Paddy Flint, at right. LOWER. The lives of American soldiers bought this victory. This is a cemetery for U.S. troops near San Stefano. American losses in this campaign totaled nearly 7,500 in 38 days of fighting.

ONE AFTER ANOTHER. This war was characterized by one campaign and fight after the other. No sooner had victory come in Sicily than preparations were being made to move on to Salerno and get that much closer to Mussolini's balconies in Rome. ABOVE. Troops of the 45th Infantry Division board LST's at Palermo for the strike that was soon to come at Salerno. Barrage balloons provide protective cover from raiding planes, particularly dive bombers.

USAAF BATTERS RUMANIAN OILFIELDS. Ploesti and its famous oilfields, covering an area of 19 square miles, were bombed for the fourth time in August, 1943. Approximately 200 Liberators and 2,000 specially-trained airmen participated in this heavy attack. It was estimated that Ploesti, 35 miles from Bucharest, supplied one-third of the fuel oil in Germany required for war purposes. The raid involved a round trip of 2,400 miles. It was executed at low level to insure accurate placement of the missiles. A total of 270,000 tons of high-explosives smashed the 13 oil refineries, pumping stations, and storage tanks causing untold damage. ABOVE. An aircraft sweeps in over the smoke stacks, against a backdrop of smoke and flame. UPPER RIGHT. Liberator bombers streak into the attack. LOWER RIGHT. A storage tank bursting into flames after a well placed hit.

THE MEDITERRANEAN THEATER

By General Mark W. Clark

AMERICAN forces first came to grips with the vaunted German "Wehrmacht" in the Mediterranean theater. There, in a series of invasions marked by a ferocity probably unsurpassed in any other area of the global war, we came to know that the armies of the so-called "master race" were indeed formidable, but not unconquerable.

It is not likely that the fierceness of the fighting around Salerno in southern Italy in the hot days of September 1943 will ever be forgotten. Neither will the amphibious landings at Anzio, the invasions in North Africa and Sicily that toppled Mussolini from his balcony, or the stubborn, wearying slugging match up the Italian mainland that enabled us to take Rome, first of the Axis capitals to fall.

For United States troops, war in the Mediterranean began on 8 November 1942 when combined American and British forces under General (then Lieutenant General Dwight D. Eisenhower) struck three portions of the northwest coast of Africa. In just three days French resistance in Morocco and Algeria had ceased, and the French took to the field with Allied forces.

Soon Allied troops under British command were pressing toward Tunisia, but in December they lost the race with the Axis to gain possession of Tunis and Bizerte. During the winter, American troops of the II Army Corps under successive commands of Generals Fredendall, Patton, and Bradley, swelled Allied strength in Tunisia. These troops had been seasoned in combat at El Guettar, Gafsa, Faid, Kasserine, Robaa, and other desert battles. Finally, in April and May, 1943, they drove eastward to take Mateur and Bizerte while British and French troops closed in on Tunis from the west and south. The result was complete rout for the vaunted Afrika Korps, which some months before had run wild and had seemed likely to seize the Suez Canal.

The remnants of this Korps, and reinforcements Hitler had rushed in to stem the Allied advance, were absolutely overwhelmed. At conclusion of this campaign, German and Italian killed and captured totaled 350,000. Moreover, many thousands of airplanes and nearly 200,000 tons of tanks, field guns and other materiel were captured.

While this rout was in progress preparations were being made to strike across the Mediterranean at Sicily and Italy from bases in North Africa. Under General Patton the U. S. Seventh Army was organized to pair off with the British Eighth Army in capturing Sicily from its German and Italian defenders. Under my command the Fifth Army was built up first to protect the Allies from an attack through Spain and Spanish Morocco, and after that menace had subsided, to carry an attack to Italy itself.

During this period troops were streaming across the Atlantic on our ever larger bridge of ships. These quickly went into advanced training for amphibious landings and the ground combat that was to come with impending attacks. Great American bases sprang up like magic. The rail and highway systems of North Africa were improved, and the heavy traffic awed the natives. All the while, Allied air power struck telling blows which choked off reinforcement and supply to the enemy in Tunisia and weakened his power to resist our planned attacks.

The first big invasion was launched on the morning of 10 July 1943, when American troops landed along the southeastern coast of Sicily from Licata to Scoglitti, and British forces struck from Cape Passero to Syracuse. All troops pressed inland to capture airfields and ports and to cut through to the northern coast. Against weak Italian resistance, but a determined German stand, the Seventh Army occupied the western portion of the island and quickly converted Palermo into an Allied port. The British met stronger opposition, but pushed on northward toward Catania. Eventually, both armies concentrated on either side of Mt. Etna, and entered Messina at about the same time on 17 August. They had driven the enemy from Sicily and inflicted great damage. The American 1st, 3rd, 9th, and 45th Infantry Divisions, 2nd Armored Division, and 82nd Airborne Division, the 1st Engineer Special Brigade, and other units had achieved, with the British Eighth Army, the capture of Sicily in 38 days from the initial landings.

This attack led to the overthrow of Mussolini on 25 July. His successor, Marshal Badoglio, proclaimed that "the war continues." However, after much hesitation, he secretly sent an emissary who signed an armistice on 3 September. General Eisenhower announced this armistice on 8 September, on the eve of the Fifth Army's attack on the mainland at Salerno.

Italy's armies ceased resistance, her fleet surrendered, and the King and Badoglio quickly left Rome. Announcement of the armistice cleared the way for our attack by eliminating Italian resistance, and it put a great strain on Hitler who was compelled to put German divisions into the areas hitherto occupied by Italians in the Balkans and Southern France. But Marshal Badoglio's hesitations and delays had enabled the Germans to place heavy reinforcements in Italy.

In the early hours of 9 September the American Fifth Army (comprising the U. S. VI Corps and British X Corps) struck at Salerno and established a beachhead. The Germans put up savage resistance, and we came dangerously close to being pushed back into the Tyrrhenian Sea. The 16th Panzer Division, already on the scene, was promptly joined by parts of five other divisions. Only by heroic effort and sacrifice was the enemy prevented from exploiting the gap which existed for a time between the U. S. 36th and British 56th Divisions. But the ground forces were fully supported in the air, and particularly by well-directed Naval gunfire. The German counter attacks of 12-14 September were repulsed, and by 15 September the beachhead was secure.

Ships poured in reinforcements. These were regrouped, and the Fifth Army, under my command, began the advance on Naples, which was captured on 1 October. With this great port in our possession it was possible to continue the drive up the Italian peninsula.

Von Vietinghoff's 10th Army though, had had time to dig in along the Volturno River, the first of a series of prepared positions at which the Germans offered bitter resistance. Fall rains turned the roads into mud and the enemy took skillful advantage of the terrain, which favored the defensive. But between 6 October and 15 November the Fifth Army forced the Germans back to their next position, the Winter Line. Heavy fighting during the worst weather forced the enemy back until by 15 January 1944 the Fifth Army (now comprising U. S. II Corps, VI Corps, French Expeditionary Corps and British X Corps) forced the enemy's strongest and best prepared position, the Gustav Line. It extended along the Garigliano and Rapido rivers, with Cassino protecting the entrance to the Liri Valley, the gateway to Rome. Repeated attempts to capture the stronghold during the winter were repulsed with heavy losses.

On 22 January we tried an end run—the amphibious attack at Anzio. A beachhead was established close to Rome, but the initial force (the VI Corps in about two-division strength) was not strong enough to capture Colli Laziali without stretching itself too thin. The Germans brought up a great number of divisions, including some from northern Italy, sealed off the beachhead, and attempted to drive the Allies back into the sea. Their most serious thrusts in mid-February were beaten back, and the beachhead was consolidated, but it had not sufficiently weakened the German forces in the Gustav Line to permit the Allies to break through there. In March the two Allied armies in Italy began preparing a new offensive.

On 11 May 1944 the Eighth Army attacked at Cassino and up the Liri Valley, while the Fifth Army thrust against the Gustav Line along a narrow front between the valley and the Tyrrhenian Sea. The French Expeditionary Corps and U. S. II Corps pushed through the mountains and unhinged the enemy line, forcing him to commit three additional divisions. At the same time the VI Corps broke out of the Anzio beachhead, captured Cisterna after a hard three-day battle, and pushed rapidly to the hills above Cori and through the Artena Gap. The VI and II Corps effected a junction in the coastal sector. Their coordinated attack on 1-2 June broke through the last defenses before Rome, which was occupied by the Fifth Army on 4 June.

The two German armies which had separated during the retreat reestablished contact and for five days held up the Fifth Army along Lake Trasimene. Enemy resistance stiffened on the approach to the Arno Valley, but on 18 July the port of Leghorn was captured. Our troops re-grouped along the valley and prepared to attack the Gothic Line, a natural position which was further strengthened by engineering works. Although the key features on each side of the Giogo Pass were captured, and the line actually breached, shortage of troops, artillery and ammunition forced a halt in operations in the mountains south of Bologna. Bad weather led to postponement of any large-scale offensive until the spring of 1945, and the men of the Fifth Army had to spend another winter in the bitter cold and snow of the Apennines.

After the 92nd Division's diversionary attack along the Legurian coast, and a thrust by the British Eighth Army from the eastern zone, the Fifth Army on 14 April launched the main effort to breach the mountain wall. The 10th Mountain Division spearheaded the attack, the IV Corps broke through the positions west of the Reno River, and the II Corps drove on to capture Bologna on 20 April. The center of the German armies was smashed south of the Po, and the Fifth Army with the 8th British Army on its right, crossed the river, fanned out, and seized the passes leading to the Alps.

By now the German force was completely beaten, bewildered and disorganized. The enemy had no way to turn, and he did what we had sought to have him do for so long—he surrendered unconditionally.

In just 19 days, after 20 dreary months, and after several bloody invasions, the final smashing offensive, supported magnificently by our air force, reduced the formidable armies of the "master race" into a disorganized welter of scattered fugitives—and the war in the Mediterranean had ended.

Frank W. Clark

ITALY FOLDS UP. By August 16, 1943, Sicily was conquered. It was a 38-day campaign, and it ended in brilliant success for the Allies. It meant disaster for Mussolini, for while a new invading armada was heading for the assault on Italy proper, Mussolini fell and Italy surrendered unconditionally on September 3. The King had selected Marshal Badoglio to replace Mussolini, and he signed an armistice with the Allies. UPPER LEFT. General Dwight D. Eisenhower, Commander in Chief of Allied Forces in the North African theater, shakes hands with General Castillani, representing Italy, after the armistice was signed at Allied Headquarters in Sicily. Maj. Gen. W. B. Smith, Eisenhower's Chief of Staff, is at left. LOWER LEFT. General Smith signing the armistice that put Mussolini on the run. Others, left to right: Commodore Dick of the British Royal Navy; Major General Rowell W. Rooks of the U.S. Army; Captain de Haan, aide to General Strong of the British Army; Lieutenant General Aldo Castillani (in civilian garb) representing the new Italian Government; and General Strong. ABOVE. Italian General Castillani affixes his signature to the armistice. Mr. Montenari (of Italy's Foreign Ministry) and General Smith stand by. This surrender was kept secret for about a week to prevent the Germans from strengthening their position in Italy before our forces could invade Salerno.

REDS REGAIN LOST TERRITORY. While American and British military successes predominated in the Mediterranean area, the Russians followed advances at Orel and Byelgorod with a six-mile push on August 6, 1943. The Germans were driven back in disorder on both the Bryansk and Kharkov fronts. The recapture of Chuguyev was succeeded by new

advances on the Bryansk front, where the Red Army regained
sixty localities including the towns of Aktinino and Novlya,
a junction of the Bryansk-Kharkov and the Bryansk-Konotop
railways. For several days the Germans launched one counter-
attack after another, using huge tank and infantry forces.
ABOVE. Russian infantrymen overwhelming a small town.

NEAR MISS ON ALLIED CONVOY. RIGHT. Allied troops of General Mark Clark's Task Force heading for the shore of Italy, watch anxiously as high-flying German planes drop bombs amidst the invasion-bound craft on September 9, 1943. The Nazi defenders used rocket bombs which left a trail of smoke as they fell and exploded immediately upon contact. After landing under enemy gunfire in which the Anglo-American forces suffered tremendous losses, the Fifth Army first deployed along a strip 30 miles long from the town of Salerno in the north to Agropoli in the south, and then began driving inland into the foothills. They penetrated 10 miles or more, capturing the town of Altavilla. The big German counter-attack opened on the night of the 13th. Waves of Nazi infantry supported by Tiger tanks swept down from the hills, bent on cutting in two the Allied beachhead and driving to the shore. Allied forces had to give way; Altavilla was lost. All day Tuesday, the 14th, the battle raged; but the Americans and English would not be driven into the water, and by the 17th the tide had turned as the U.S. Fifth and British Eighth Armies made their juncture. Germany had lost her fight for Southern Italy. Salerno itself was now permanently cleared of Germans, and the Fifth Army overran the Sorrentine Peninsula to the northwest, liberating the town of Amalfi along with many other beautiful resort towns on the Tyrrhenian coast. For the first time, the Allies enjoyed a continuous unbroken line from one coast of Italy to the other. Their next goal was Naples. General Mark Clark, who led the Fifth and Eighth Armies into Salerno, was highly commended for his leadership in the Salerno campaign. ABOVE. The General reviews maps with Admiral J. K. Hewitt in the chart room of their command ship en route to Salerno, while troops converged in landing craft.

ITALIAN FLEET SURRENDERS. On the morning of September 11, Admiral Cunningham announced in an official statement that "the Italian battle fleet is now anchored under the guns of Malta." After the representatives of Marshal Badoglio had signed an armistice with the Allies three days previously, units of the Italian fleet left Taranto, Spezia, and various other ports and sailed for Malta, where they arrived on September 10, flying the Italian colors and the black pennants which were the agreed marks of identification. Four Italian battleships, six cruisers, and seven destroyers arrived at Malta that day; four Italian admirals were with their ships. The convoy was heavily bombed by German Stukas and torpedo-bombers in the straits between Corsica and Sardinia in an attempt to prevent the ships from reaching Malta. Before she could be provided with Allied air cover, the battleship "Roma" was sunk by a direct hit which split her in two. Survivors were picked up by other Italian warships. Heavy and accurate Italian anti-aircraft fire soon drove off the German planes. A huge gathering including Admiral Cunningham and General Eisenhower watched the Italian Fleet enter Valetta. Messages of congratulations were sent to Admiral Cunningham by King George VI, the Board of Admiralty, and General Eisenhower. Admiral Cunningham said, "These ships now added to our strength are first class; and now that the Mediterranean is cleared it will release many ships for use against the Japanese." Italian submarines kept appearing from various ports and two days after the main Italian fleet had arrived at Malta it was joined by the battleship "Giulio Cesare," which had steamed all the way from Venice to join the Allies. On September 12, seven additional battleships arrived in the Balearics, five of which were interned for overstaying the 24 hours permitted in a neutral port. Other units surrendered in Bone, Algeria. LEFT. A portion of the Italian Fleet is photographed steaming toward Valetta, Malta.

THE AVALANCHE. On September 8, 1943, countless ships loaded with Allied troops and the equipment it takes to win a war sailed from ports in Sicily and North Africa. Their destination was Salerno in southern Italy—an area which Mr. Churchill termed "the soft underbelly" of Axis territory. In the midst of this relatively short voyage came the announcement from General Eisenhower that the Italians had capitulated and thrown in the towel. Troops in scores of ships cheered when they heard this news. UPPER LEFT. Elements of the 143rd Infantry Regiment, Salerno-bound, get the word and kick up a fuss about it somewhere on the Mediterranean on September 8, the day before they were to hit the beach. LOWER LEFT. A portion of the invasion fleet nears the Italian shore below Salerno under a protective smoke screen laid down by U. S. and British destroyers. First troops hit the beach between 3 and 4 o'clock on the morning of September 9. Anyone who thought this was going to be easy — and many did, because of Italy's surrender—were due for a bitter disappointment. Germans had discovered the convoys, taken over Italian defenses along the coast, rushed in troops, and were ready for the assault. With mortars and their dreaded 88's they poured a withering fire into the invaders in both the American and British sectors of the beach. UPPER RIGHT. Members of the 143rd Infantry Regiment Combat Team dash from their landing boats to the shore on D-Day. LOWER RIGHT. Casualties grew by leaps and bounds as the Germans attempted to throw us back into the sea. Here a wounded soldier is carried to a landing craft that will take him to a hospital ship standing by near the beaches.

MUSSOLINI RELEASED BY GERMANS. Since the overthrow
of the former Italian dictator on July 24, 1943, he had been
kept a prisoner in the Gran Sasso Hotel in the Abruzzi
Mountains north of Rome. On September 12, Radio Berlin
announced that German paratroopers and S.S. men had
"carried out an operation for the liberation of Mussolini."
Two years later, the latter was to suffer an ignominious end
when he was assassinated, along with his mistress, by en-
raged Italian partisans and hung up by his heels in a square
in Milan. ABOVE. Mussolini bids farewell to his "liberator."

SEEING THE SIGHTS. If given a preference the average
American soldier would much rather have stayed at home.
Nevertheless, his travels and experience carried him to
many lands and enabled him to see many sights he would
probably never have seen otherwise. ABOVE. A soldier
admires a religious statue in the midst of the rubble war
brought to Cologne. The spires of famous Cologne Cathedral
were relatively unhurt, due to U.S. "pinpoint bombing."

OPERATION STRANGLE. UPPER. In the spring of 1944 there were 18 Axis divisions in the central Italian area. It was the job of the 12th and 15th Air Forces to knock out bridges, smash up rail centers, attack motor trucks, etc., to choke off their supplies. B-25s and two P-47s fly over a wrecked road bridge in the Brenner Pass. LOWER. Early in 1945 a similar "strangle" operation was applied on a greater scale in western Germany by the 8th Air Force and RAF. The Hohenzollern Bridge near Cologne was heavily damaged in an attack by the 8th.

THE BEACH IS HELD. Despite everything the Germans threw at the invaders, the beach was held. On September 11 the Hermann Goering Panzer Division and other armored forces launched a bitter counter attack against the Allies, but it was finally repulsed by September 17 by ground troops, supported by Naval gunfire and elements of the Allied air forces. UPPER. Elements of Company C, 143rd Infantry, ready to advance from Red Beach on D-Day. LOWER. Infantry troops, mopping up, cautiously enter the town of Acerno, Italy, on September 22.

NAPLES FALLS. After securing its beachhead the American Fifth Army under command of Lieutenant General (now General) Mark W. Clark pushed toward Naples and occupied that city on October 1, 1943. UPPER LEFT. Headquarters company of the 505th Parachute Regiment entering Naples on October 2. LOWER LEFT. Welcomed by Latins, American troops advance through Naples on October 3. The arrow points to Rome, destination of the Allies. ABOVE. General Clark, with Maj. Gen. Gruenther and Lt. Col. Ryan, presents Monsignor Francesco Cuzzo with a sum of money collected in Fifth Army Headquarters to pay for damage done to his monastery by a shell.

DESTRUCTION AT NAPLES. The Germans demolished Naples before evacuating it. They destroyed the water supply, mined buildings and razed port facilities with their usual degree of thoroughness. UPPER LEFT. What was left of a section of the Naples waterfront area after Allied bombings and the Germans had done their work. LOWER LEFT. Lieutenant Colonel Arthur Sutherland, General Clark and British officers study the situation at the front. This picture was made in Naples October 19 as the enemy retreated to the north and prepared to make a stand. ABOVE. Battle-weary troops of the 168th Infantry, 34th Division, advance resolutely toward Alifo, Italy, on October 23.

BATTLEFIELD IN
THE MEDITERRANEAN SKIES

By Major General Lauris Norstad

THE contribution of Air Power to Mediterranean victory can be summarized statistically—so many tons of bombs dropped, so many enemy aircraft shot down. It can be summarized by the long list of campaigns won—Tunisia, Pantelleria, Ploesti, and so on. But over and above the bombs dropped and the battles won, the Air Forces in the Mediterranean made two great contributions to the Allied cause everywhere; for here was the primary crucible for the development of tactical air power and here occurred the evolution of joint command between Allies.

Combined command had its longest, most comprehensive and most consecutive history in the Mediterranean Theater. When the North African campaign began, Allied air forces were three separate entities. In November 1942, in addition to Air Marshal Coningham's predominately RAF Tactical Air Force which was moving west from El Alamein, an American air force was arriving in western Algeria and Morocco and an RAF command landed in the Algiers area. Coningham's force had demonstrated without question the importance of an integrated tactical air force which acted as a whole. Unity of command, which was accepted at the Casablanca Conference, solved the problem of combining an independent RAF with AAF units subordinate to the Army by designating an RAF officer to be Allied Air Commander for Mediterranean operations.

The history of the air forces in the Mediterranean falls naturally into three phases. The first phase began at El Alamein with the RAF Desert Air Force and at Casablanca and Oran with the embryo Twelfth, and ended when both converged in Tunisia and joined under General Spaatz's command as the Northwest African Air Forces. The career of the Mediterranean Air Command, assembling all the various Allied air forces in the Mediterranean under one management for the first time, comprised the second phase. With mounting strength, Mediterranean Air Command and Northwest Africa Air Forces combined in an operational command post to conduct the Tunisian campaign, the invasion of Sicily, and the conquest of Southern Italy as far north as Cassino. The third phase extended from the creation of the Mediterranean Allied Air Forces in December 1943, until enemy forces surrendered in May 1945.

Adapting the air-ground tactics of El Alamein, the Twelfth Air Force strove for complete air superiority over the enemy. Interdiction of German supply lines to Tunisia was the next selected objective, and this was accomplished by bombing ports, sinking ships, and shooting down the aerial convoys which Germany used as a desperate last resort to strengthen her African forces. Close support of ground troops in the final break-through was its third operation as a tactical force.

The same pattern was repeated in Sicily and then in Southern Italy. The spectacular strafing of 200 German bombers at Foggia enabled the Salerno beachhead to be established without significant air opposition. And when the Salerno battle was at its crisis, Allied forces mustered more than 1,000 air sorties daily for two days in succession, an unprecedented effort that assisted in halting enemy counter-attack.

With the movement of the war away from North Africa onto the Italian mainland, the air structure needed reorganization.

Created in December, the Mediterranean Allied Air Forces within a few months achieved full strength, especially in heavy bombers. Its combined aircraft flew 54,000 sorties to support landing troops at Anzio, and one month later played an important part in stopping the German counter-attack that threatened to push the beachhead back into the sea.

The capture of the air bases on the plaines of Foggia in the early stages of the Italian campaign may go down in military annals as one of the keys to the liberation of Europe, for it was from that "soft underbelly" that the strategic heavy bombers were based which helped destroy Hitler's war machine. Even before the activation of the Fifteenth U.S. Strategic Air Force, Flying Fortresses and Liberators were using Foggia as a staging area for flights to targets beyond the range of bombers based in England.

The Fifteenth Air Force was activated November 1, 1943, and the next day flew its first mission, bombarding the Messerschmitt fighter plants at Wiener Neustadt, Austria. It was obvious from the beginning that the success of strategic operations depended on air superiority providing freedom for our heavy bombers to range over enemy territory. Germany had converted its aircraft industry to fighter production and moved it as far from the Britain-based threat as possible—to Bavaria, Austria, and Hungary. The Fifteenth Air Force, like the Eighth, had to knock the "Luftwaffe" from the air while attacking the Nazi war machine. In its first year, 3,635 aircraft fell before the fire power of the bombers and fighter escorts, and 2,016 more enemy aircraft were destroyed while still on the ground.

Carefully integrated with the Eighth Air Force and the RAF Bomber Command in England, attacks by the Fifteenth ranged from southern France through Germany, Poland, Czechoslovakia and the Balkans. Milestone in operations was the execution of the first shuttle mission to Russia, bombing Hungarian railyards en route to Soviet bases. But undoubtedly the most significant achievement of the Strategic Air Force was the battle of Ploesti—the number one oil target in Europe.

The destruction of Ploesti oil between April and August, 1944, was part of a comprehensive program directed toward the systematic liquidation of all major Nazi oil production centers. There were still 21 crude and synthetic oil targets in Mediterranean Allied Air Forces territory after Ploesti's fall, and these were the particular province of Fifteenth AAF heavies. By mid-March 1945, only six were operating, and by April, production of Axis oil was 10 per cent what it had been at the start of the campaign one year previously.

The most significant demonstration not only of what tactical air power could do in a decisive air-ground offensive, but what it should do, was reached in Operation DIADEM, the great combined air and land action which began on May 12, 1944, when Allied foot soldiers surged forward into action from Cassino to the sea and in six weeks caused German withdrawal to the Pisa-Rimini line. Considering the previous stalemate of the Italian campaign, this was a resounding military feat.

Air superiority was essential—and we had it. By the time DIADEM proper was under way, the "Luftwaffe" was able to fly only 700 sorties in the first week of battle as against 20,000 sorties flown by the Mediterranean Allied Air Forces.

Out of the Italian campaign came this conclusion, established more firmly than ever and later proved again in France: "that in the absence of an effective enemy air force, the primary role of tactical air power is to operate against enemy supply lines in the rear rather than in the immediate battle area." When General Montgomery and Air Marshal Coningham used their small air force in North Africa to nip Rommel's tenuous and over-extended supply lines—cutting roads, downing air transports, sinking ships, and strafing motorized transport all the way from Alamein to Tunis, they provided the first real proof of the wisdom of this doctrine.

Attacks on Italian marshalling yards were the major means of disrupting the enemy's flow of supplies. But, although these yards were soon blasted into uselessness, the tracks between them still carried materiel to the foe. As it was imperative that all rail lines be cut, quickly and simultaneously the AAF went ahead with its plans for daylight precision bombing of "small" targets as well as the marshalling yards. By the time Operation STRANGLE (the "aerial" offensive immediately preceding the joint air-ground DIADEM) began, "bridge-busting" poli-

cies had been adopted and a concerted program to knock out all German communications was on. Within a few weeks' time the enemy began to gasp for breath, becoming short of gasoline, ammunition, and food.

In terms of effort, operations STRANGLE and DIADEM were expensive, totalling together 137,949 effective sorties and the expenditure of 84,603 tons of bombs. In terms of aircraft losses, however, the campaigns were economical beyond hope. Mediterranean Allied Air Forces lost a total of only 803 planes or about one-half of one percent of total effective sorties.

During the early spring of 1945, German General Kesselring began devious surrender negotiations for his Italy-based forces. He was, however, recalled to the Western Front in mid-March and negotiations broke down with his successor, Von Vietinghoff, who planned to pull back into Austria. Our air power had isolated the battle area by the "bridge-busting" pattern over the Po River and the Brenner Pass, and was readied for operations in close support of ground forces. We had an effective combat strength of 4,393 planes against 130 of the once overwhelming "Luftwaffe."

In April 1945, Fifteenth AAF heavies carpet-bombed in front of the Eighth Army with 1,692 tons of fragmentation bombs. Accuracy was rated "superb." Late that afternoon, the British Eighth Army attacked across the Senio River. Next day, heavies again carpet-bombed, dropping 1,792 tons. On the 14th the U.S. Fifth Army attacked southwest of Bologna to be assisted the following day by 1,235 heavy bombers. From then on there was no stopping the Allied advance. Backed up against the bridgeless Po, the Germans left practically all of their heavy equipment and swam across. Beyond the Po, there was no organized enemy resistance. In three weeks, fighters and fighter-bombers destroyed 4,226 motor transport vehicles and damaged 4,401. The Germans disintegrated, divisions and corps surrendering en masse. By the end of April, there were 137,000 German prisoners, and on May 2nd, General Von Vietinghoff surrendered his remaining forces.

For the Mediterranean Allied Air Forces the war was over. It and its predecessor organizations had dispatched 1,178,243 sorties since the opening of the North African campaign in November 1942, had dropped 674,195 tons of bombs, shot down 8,721 enemy aircraft, and destroyed 4,888 on the ground. And—for victory it had paid the price of 9,347 planes, and 3,863 American airmen known to have been killed in action.

THE MOSCOW CONFERENCE. An attempt was made in November, 1943, to join the hands of Russia, Britain, and the United States as a means of ending the war with Germany and winning the peace. The meeting was presided over by the heads of foreign affairs of the three countries: Molotov, Eden, and Hull. It was agreed that the three Allies establish a European Advisory Commission in London. This body was to study the post-war political problems of Europe and to make appropriate recommendations to the governments. (In 1943 the Allied world had rejoiced at the significance of the conference. It was to have ended a quarter century of distrust between Russia and the Western powers; a distrust dating back to 1917 when Allied troops invaded Russia to combat the Bolshevist movement, and one that had flared anew in 1938 when the U.S.S.R. was excluded from the Munich Conference.) In early 1944, the Commission worked in London and agreed on recommendations for future surrender terms for Germany and upon national zones of occupation. Here (upper), signing the pact originally drafted to "cement" relations with Russia and the West are, left to right, Fu Ping-sheung, Chinese Ambassador; Secretary of State Cordell Hull; V. M. Molotov, Soviet Commissar of Foreign Affairs, and Anthony Eden, British Minister of Foreign Affairs. LOWER. Secretary Hull, accompanied by Molotov, reviews an honor guard of hand-picked Russian troops.

UP THE BOOT. The Allied drive up the rugged Italian boot was a tough slugging match in the winter of 1943-44. Rains had turned the roads into mud, and the enemy took advantage of the terrain. But between October 6 and November 15 the Fifth Army had forced the enemy back from the Volturno to his next position, the Winter Line. UPPER. Working on shore and in swollen waters of the Volturno these Army Engineers set up a bridge November 19. LOWER. Troops of Company G, 2nd Battalion, 141st Infantry Regiment, are shown in the San Vittore area after attacking Mt. Irocchio.

CAIRO CONFERENCE. Generalissimo Chiang Kai-shek, President Roosevelt and Prime Minister Churchill are shown (above) as they met in Egypt during the last week of November, 1943, to plan the ultimate offensives against the Axis, and to decide the disposition of Japan, particularly, following capitulation. The three, accompanied by 300 of the top war leaders of their nations, hoped to reshape the future of the Orient. One of the largest empires ever put together, Japan, was doomed at the conference. In fifty years the Japanese had brought a large portion of the human race under their domination along with territory covering approximately 3,000,000 square miles. Now the three leaders determinedly pledged their nations to strip away these conquests, and to drive the Nipponese back into their home lands. Ultimately it was hoped to compress the Japanese Empire into an area no larger than the State of California, and to reduce the former to the status of a third-rate power. Thus Japan's ability to wage war would be wiped out automatically, as she would lose the indispensable raw materials acquired from Manchuria and the South Seas, plus the island bases imperative to provide her fleet with long-range striking power. The Generalissimo, who spoke only Chinese, brought his famed wife as his interpreter. She was the only woman present within the inner circle of the conference. As for China, herself, the Cairo Conference came as a life-giving tonic. For the first time since medieval days, the country was formally recognized as one of the great powers of the world, in status of full equality. Eventually, she would be freed from Japan's armed tutelage, and presumably from Occidental pressure as well. The long, arduous war against Japan, dating from 1937, had brought China to the point of exhaustion.

COMMANDER-IN-CHIEF HONORS ALLIED COMMAND-
ER. President Roosevelt is shown (above) as he awarded
the Legion of Merit to General Dwight D. Eisenhower during the General's visit to the conference of Roosevelt,
Churchill and Stalin. The ceremony took place at Teheran
where the Conference was held. It was during the sessions
at Teheran and Cairo that the decision to appoint General
Eisenhower as the Allied Commander-in-Chief was made.

RADAR BOMBING THROUGH OVERCAST. All of Europe was covered with a cloud blanket on December 13, 1943. Yet on that day the 8th Air Force sent out the greatest number of bombers yet to take off from England in the daytime, a record 10-wing mission of more than 740 B-17s and B-24s against Kiel, Bremen, and Hamburg. The force was led by "Mickey," AAF nickname for the radar search set APS-15, technically known as H_2X. This badweather bombsight was originally installed only in the lead "pathfinder" plane of the lead Group of each Wing.

RAZING THE NAZI CAPITAL. On the night of December 16, British planes, after 13 nights of respite, dropped more than 1,500 tons of bombs on Berlin in addition to thousands of incendiaries. Thirty bombers were lost during the attack. This was the 96th air attack directed against Berlin since the outbreak of hostilities. In a daylight raid the same day American planes attacked the German port of Emden. ABOVE. As this "bomb bay view" of a factory district indicates, the unwelcome British missiles are finding their mark.

OUTWITTING THE NAZIS. Retreating Nazis intended to clog the Allied advance with this and other ships sunk in Naples harbor. When U. S. Army engineers eyed this hulk, however, they recognized an asset. Quickly they gauged its position near the blasted docks, tested its stability. Satisfied it was stuck fast, they threw up a bridge and enabled full-scale docking operations to be carried out on the barnacle-studded hull. All five hatches of the Liberty ship shown moored alongside are being unloaded at once. Guns, clothes and food flow to Allied forces clawing their way up Italy's spiny terrain. Much of the Corps of Engineers' efforts to keep supply lines open lifted few eyebrows save those of experts in logistics. Here the ability of the Army's builders to improvise, points up their deeds in spectacular fashion. Systematic destruction of ports, bridges, roads and railways challenged the engineers throughout the entire Italian campaign.

ALLIES ON ROADS TO ROME. Like a stocking being drawn inch by inch up an inflamed leg, Allied forces advanced in Italy. On the map (above), battle lines can be seen at four stages reached since Montgomery's forces crossed the Strait of Messina. From the Anzio beachhead it was planned to drive eastward to sever the Appian Way and the Via Cassina, the Germans' two main arteries to the front. Weather intervened. In January, 1944, each side bogged down in wet cold which alternately froze and soaked men, equipment, and the battered land they fought for.

TRESPASSING ON "MARE NOSTRUM." An American soldier peers over the stern of his ship at units of an Allied invasion fleet dotting the Tyrrhenian Sea. These craft bear arms and men toward Anzio, the battleground which shortly was to flare into one of the war's bloodiest. Expecting deadly opposition to first landing attempts, Allied forces encountered only a few thunderstruck garrison troops. But four days later, units of two German divisions had wheeled into position on both shallow Allied flanks. German planes soon skimmed these waters to strafe approaching ships.

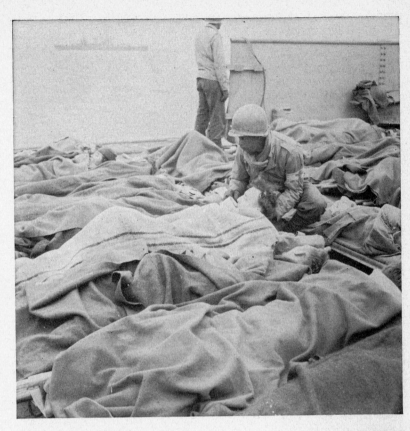

END RUN. After months of struggling in foul weather the Fifth Army had, by January 15, 1944, pushed the Germans from their Winter Line back to the Gustav Line, their next prepared position. At this time the Fifth Army included the United States II Corps, French Expeditionary Corps, and the British X Corps. These troops now found it impossible to take the German stronghold of Cassino. In order to skirt Gustav Line entrenchments, the Allies hit the beaches of Anzio and Nettuno on January 22. They found them lightly defended. Hurriedly the Allies massed men and equipment on shore with which to strengthen their hold. In a few days the area had been surrounded by German heavy artillery. From high vantage points, shells rained day and night into the tiny patch of land. But neither shellfire nor determined thrusts by German infantry were able to chase the Allies back to the sea. Once the beachhead was consolidated, however, it was months before it could be exploited as a base from which to menace German supply lines to the main front. And all this time the Gustav Line failed to give at any point, despite the Germans' having transferred units of two divisions to Anzio. UPPER LEFT. D-Day at Anzio, with troops and equipment slogging ashore during low tide. Smoke erupts from a burning LCI. LOWER LEFT. "Ducks" and other equipment churn through the water and roll inland. UPPER RIGHT. A medic of the 52nd Medical Battalion gives a drink to one of the thousands of men wounded at Anzio. These casualties are on their way to a hospital ship. LOWER RIGHT. A British 4.5 gun spurts flame in the night. With a range of about 21,000 yards, these "Long Toms" effectively buttressed the Allied stand. Yet when this picture was snapped on March 17, 1944, the Germans still clung stiffly to their positions around the beachhead, within which occurred some of the most concentrated combat encountered during the war.

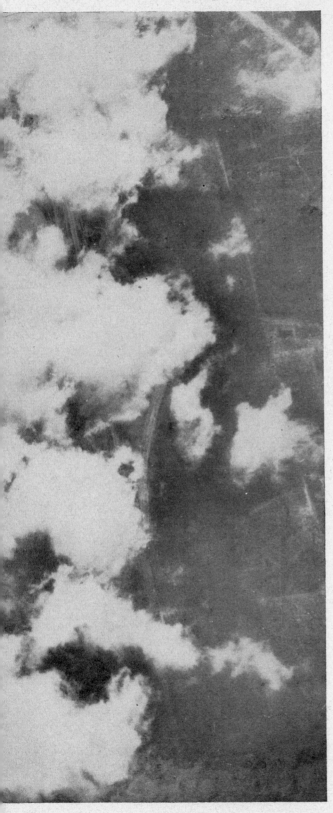

FORTRESSES HIT IN DAYLIGHT. American Flying Fortresses dropped bombs on Berlin in daylight for the first time on March 4, 1944, while other groups of American heavy bombers raided targets in Eastern Germany. Fourteen American bombers and twenty-six fighters failed to return from this mission. Approximately forty German planes rose to intercept the raiders over the capital city. This round-trip flight of 1,200 miles from British bases was made in temperatures as low as 76 degrees below zero, amid blinding snowstorms. The weight of bombs dropped was only a sample of the loads to come. Prior to this U.S. raid, the Royal Air Force had dumped 32,000 tons of explosives into Berlin. Heavy and medium bombers had carried out ninety-five raids to do this. Since the Battle of Berlin began on November 18, 1943, R.A.F. bombers had made more than fifteen major attacks and had dropped 23,000 tons of bombs. This amounted to more than three times the weight hurled at London during the entire blitz of 1940-1941. With the Americans now taking to the air in the daytime, the Battle of Berlin was on in earnest. In the picture (left), hits are registered on a rayon and textile plant in the Wittenberg district, southwest of Berlin.

AN ITALIAN TOWN CRUMBLES. While Allied Forces gained against the Japs, other Americans and their Allies slugged it out with Germans on the other side of the world in Italy. General Mark Clark's drive for Rome bogged down in the winter of 1944, but in the spring his forces regrouped and renewed the assault on Cassino, bastion of the Gustav Line. Italy witnessed some of the bitterest combat of the war. Salerno and Anzio had been especially tough. Now Cassino called on all the shells and fortitude the Allies could muster. The only way to root out the Germans was to reduce the pitiable town to a heap of smashed stone and concrete. UPPER LEFT. Preceding the assault on Cassino, members of the 36th Field Artillery Regiment fire a 155 mm rifle in the Mt. Camino area. LOWER LEFT. Thick smoke boils over Cassino during terrifically concentrated air attack. UPPER RIGHT. "Hangman's Hill" towers over the ruins. LOWER RIGHT. A closer view of "Hangman's Hill" with a GI standing amid the debris, after the six-day push. Teamwork by Allied troops was nowhere better utilized than at Cassino, with American, British, French and Polish troops converging. Rome was now open.

MOVING UP AGAIN. After a winter in which dry socks meant the difference between comfort and misery, and in which our forces scarcely knew whether they were gaining or losing ground, the advance recrudesced as U.S. troops sped up the coast from the Minturno toward Anzio. Meantime the U.S. VI Corps broke out of the Anzio beachhead area itself and drove for Cisterna. Here they caught up with those Germans who had penned them in the beachhead area since January. By the time Cisterna fell the Allies had caught the scent of victory and were not to be checked before rolling through Rome. The Germans still begrudged every square foot but had lost their ally—bad weather. Two newly arrived Yank divisions, the 85th and the 88th, experienced combat for the first time in this campaign. Against stout resistance they acquitted themselves with the skill and tenacity of veterans. UPPER. Men of the 339th Regiment, 85th Division, prowl through the Scauri area with eyes and ears alert. Their job was to root out every sniper crouched in the hills and battered houses. LOWER. Troops of the same regiment tramp northward on the road from Formia to Itri. They were soon to see Rome.

THE SELECTEES. In his final report to the Secretary of War as Chief of Staff, General Marshall had high praise for the fighting qualities of the selectee troops of the 88th and 85th Divisions. These units, activated in December, 1941, and composed almost entirely of selectees, fought as veterans on their first combat assignments in Italy. The General declared their action was confirmation of the soundness of division activation and training programs initiated early in the war. UPPER. American soldiers enter Itri on May 19. LOWER. Fifth Army troops move through the town of Fondi May 21.

THE ETERNAL CITY. After the Gustav Line, Cassino and Cisterna, "the eternal city" of Rome was next. This first of the Axis capitals to fall was entered by elements of the Fifth Army on June 4, just two days before the Normandy landings. UPPER LEFT. Members of the 1st Special Force and 351st Infantry, 88th Division, entering the outskirts of Rome on June 4. These were among the first troops to see the Italian capital. LOWER LEFT. There was not much time to see the sights. Most troops pushed on through after the retreating Germans. These Fifth Army men are not tarrying on June 5. ABOVE. While Italians stare, Fifth Army vehicles pass the ancient Coliseum as they begin to occupy Rome.

ITALIAN CAPITAL IS FREED. Crowds in Rome forget business to greet top-ranking Allied officers as they arrive. A girl gratefully clasps the hand of General Mark W. Clark, Commander of Allied forces in Italy. With the General are Major General Alfred M. Gruenther, his Chief-of-Staff, Major General Geoffrey Keyes, Commander of the 2nd Corps of the Fifth Army, and the driver, Tech. Sergeant Holden.

A GI KEEPS A PROMISE. An American soldier of the triumphant Fifth Army imitates Benito Mussolini on the balcony of
the Palazzo Venezia. From here, with the emblems of Fascism
decked lavishly about him and with loudspeakers thundering
every bellow, the heavy-jawed dictator once harangued a
nation. The story goes that the GI had promised friends at
home that he would pose on the famous balcony in Rome.

THE INVASION OF
NORMANDY

By Vice Admiral Alan G. Kirk, USN

TO MANY Americans the expression "D-day" means but one thing—June 6, 1944. It was on that day that the greatest aggregation of land, sea and air forces ever assembled hurled themselves against the Normandy coast and struck the combined blow that was the beginning of the end for the Nazi military machine.

As early as January 1943, the Combined Chiefs of Staffs at the Casablanca Conference had projected this invasion. Almost from the beginning military leaders everywhere had realized that, regardless of Russian victories or long-range bombing, sooner or later the German fortress of Europe would have to be invaded and the Nazis decisively beaten on their own soil before complete victory could be achieved.

That resistance would be bitter had already been proved in the Allied commando raid on Dieppe in 1942, which resulted in almost complete annihilation of the attacking troops. The outer fringes of the bastion of Europe were studded with steel and concrete, beach obstacles, and mines. From Wilhelmshaven to Bordeaux enemy troops and millions of political slaves had labored four frantic years, pouring the concrete and digging the caves, making the "western wall" of Europe the most formidable barrier ever known to fighting man. The Germans themselves called it "impregnable."

Early in 1943 advance units of the U.S. Navy amphibious forces began to arrive in the British Isles to prepare the stage for the Invasion. After establishment of "Base 1" in Ireland, our sailors and Seabees began the construction of other bases in England as "jumping off" points for the great attack. "Base 2" was in Scotland; then came amphibious bases at Pernarth and Milford Haven in Wales, at Falmouth and Plymouth, at Poole and Weymouth and Southampton and Fowey. At every cove and bay which could conceivably be used for harboring and loading naval vessels, the Royal Navy and the U.S. Navy set up installations and began readying the landing craft and transports which were to carry our troops to the shores of the enemy. Intensive training operations were instituted in every phase of amphibious warfare from boat-handling to gas-mask drills. In January 1944, General Eisenhower arrived in England to take supreme command of all the invasion forces. By March had begun the three months of continuous pounding by the U.S. 8th Air Force, the U.S. 9th Air Force, and the Royal Air Force at targets along the coast and in northern France, the Low Countries, and Western Germany.

WHEN AND WHERE

EVERYONE knew what was coming—even the Germans. But what only a few men in all the world knew was "where" the blow would come and "when" it would come. The answers to those questions were among the most closely guarded secrets of the entire war, and were known only to a few of the highest commanders in the Allied forces. As D-day approached, the air attacks were intensified. Actual loading of assault troops began on June 1. The men were briefed and the ships "sealed," and the great armada hung poised on the southern coast of Britain, waiting only for the final "this is it" message from Supreme Allied Headquarters.

D-day had originally been set as June 5, but due to adverse weather conditions there was a last postponement of 24-hours. Then on the night of June 5, our last-minute air attacks rose to a crescendo, paratroopers made their jumps far inland, and the great armada moved across the Channel. And for the next 24 hours the fate of Europe perhaps lay in the hands of the United States and Royal Navies.

But almost every contingency had been anticipated in a masterpiece of far-sighted planning. From long months before, things had been figured to the last inch and last second. A fleet of 4,000 ships, converging from half the points of the compass, and of varying sizes and varying speeds, reached the rendezvous with split-second timing. And from that point on, all those vessels continued to operate with split-second timing.

THE LANDING

THE site selected for the landing was a stretch of beach on the Normandy coast between the Seine and halfway up the Cotentin Peninsula. British troops were to land on the eastern beaches, and American troops on the western beaches. Complete direction of the operation while crossing the Channel lay in the hands of the naval commanders: Rear Admiral Alan G. Kirk, USN, commanded the U.S. Naval forces and Admiral Sir Philip Vian, RN, commanded the British Naval forces.

Minesweepers were already far ahead, sweeping channels right in to the beach and dropping lighted buoys to mark the swept channels. Reference vessels were posted at every turn in the courses, to guide traffic into the proper lanes. Inside the 1,000-yard line off shore special control vessels would guide the assault boats in the final dash.

All across the Channel the great armada stretched, with the battleships, cruisers, and destroyers guarding the van and the flanks. A veritable umbrella of air coverage gave protection against air attack. Air patrols as well as surface vessels kept down any U-boat that might venture near. Then the bombardment ships moved in and began hurling an avalanche of shells against the surprised Nazi pillboxes, entrenchments, and gun emplacements. The old U.S. battleship "Texas" opened fire at 12,000 yards; the old "Arkansas" moved in to 6,000 yards—a bare three miles. The destroyers delivered their fire at such close range that, as one observer put it, "they had their bows against the beach." That avalanche of shells beat down German 88's and 105's high up on the bluffs above Omaha Beach; it hammered the concrete gun emplacements amid the dunes and swampland of Utah Beach.

Then the transports, reaching the Transport Area, lowered their assault craft, the LCVP's and LCM's; the troops swarmed down, and the amphibious craft chugged off toward shore with their loads. Already, ahead of them, the Navy and Army demolition teams were driving in through the shallow water, blowing up underwater obstacles under a hail of enemy bullets. Too, enemy mobile 88's and 105's and other Nazi guns which had lain outside the zone of fire of the bombardment vessels, began to open up with a heavy crossfire, and casualties were heavy. Offshore vessels were struck, to flame up or lie helpless and sinking. Now the U.S. Coast Guard rescue craft, especially equipped and trained, plunged in under the fire and made sensational rescues as they pulled men from the water or from sinking wrecks. Then bombers and ships' gun fire searched out the hidden guns and put them permanently out of commission.

THE FIRST DAY

BY LATE afternoon our troops had secured the landing beaches. At the end of the first 24 hours, 66,000 troops had been landed on the two American beaches; at the end of seven days, al-most 250,000 Americans were ashore. The supply ships were now moving across a steady stream of supplies, ammunition, and reinforcements. Blockships were sunk to form breakwaters in the open roads. The secret "Mulberries" — huge floating harbors constructed in sections and towed across— were assembled to form the long piers so necessary for the countless supplies needed for the drive through France and Germany. By September 1, over 2,000,000 men, 440,000 vehicles, and 2,480,000 tons of stores had been landed by the Allies, and all but a small portion of them had gone in over the beaches.

For the ultimate battle of Germany, however, permanent harbors were needed. Cherbourg offered an ideal solution, but Cherbourg remained in Nazi hands. And to Cherbourg's previously powerful defenses the Nazis had in four years added tremendous strength. Driving across the peninsula, our ground troops attacked Cherbourg from the rear. From the Channel our naval forces attacked the seaward side. Against the enormous coast defense guns in the land of forts of Cherbourg our battleships and cruisers and destroyers matched their own naval guns. Down they swept, in plain view of the coast, and with amazing skill dropped their shells on enemy gun emplacements with pinpoint accuracy. With their forts beaten down around their ears, the Nazis finally surrendered. And the U.S. Navy at Cherbourg as well as at Normandy had proved that what had been regarded for two hundred years as a military axiom was just another fallacy—i.e., that naval ships cannot engage on equal terms with strong coast defense guns in permanent fortifications. The U.S. Navy had not only engaged the Nazi land fortresses on equal terms, they had overwhelmed them with superior gunfire.

Alan Kirk

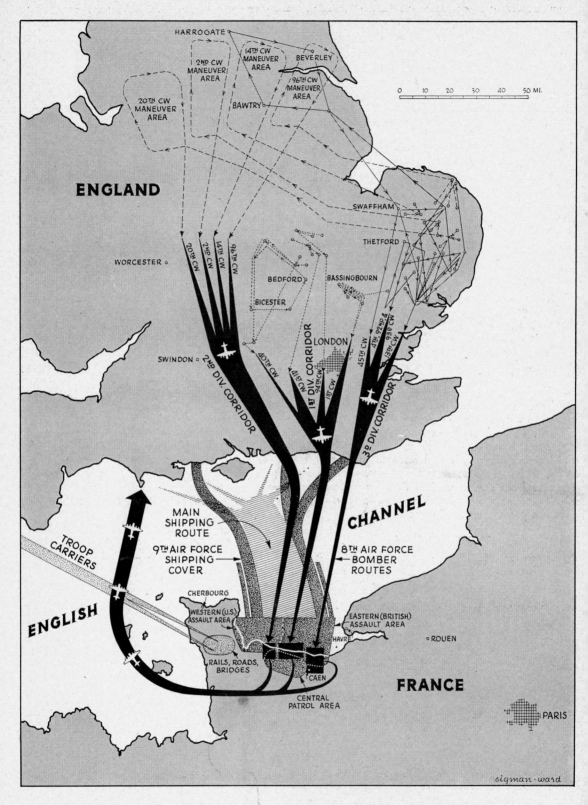

AAF's role: Black arrows show routes of 8th AF heavy bombers in Normandy invasion.
Heavy shaded corridors show those of 9th AF bombers.

REAL PROPERTY VALUES. For sheer destruction, there was never a war that equaled the last one. When Hitler brought the wrath of the world down on Germany by his aggression he brought its destruction. UPPER. What was left of Cologne. LOWER. A flame-throwing tank, which brought terror and death to countless Japanese on the long road back to the Philippines, goes into action. Such tanks were particularly effective for routing the Japs from their numerous caves. Such American ingenuity in providing our fighting men with better weapons saved a great many lives.

EASTER EGGS FOR HITLER. Ordnance men of a B-24 Group, 15th Air Force in Italy, set to work with paint and brush to design Easter "specials" for a Nazi aircraft factory in Austria, April 1944. In its blasting of industrial targets in the rugged, mountainous terrain of southern Europe, the 15th achieved a brilliant record. At the end of the first year (Nov. 1944) its planes had flown a total of 150,000,000 miles to hit 620 targets in 12 different countries.

BUILDING UP THE BEACHHEAD. LCI's, hospital ships, tugs, and naval ships bombarding coastal gun emplacements—all shapes and sizes of sea-craft added their bit for the embattled troops digging in ashore. Chaotic as it appears, this traffic is running on schedule. Another reason for the early success of the Normandy invasion was complete Allied control of the water between England and France. German subs ducked out of sight of roving naval planes.

D-DAY. This is what the German-held coast of France looked like to Allied soldiers as they resolutely swarmed from their landing barges in the face of fierce enemy fire on the fateful day of 6 June 1944. Heavily-laden with their combat and

field equipment, the men waded waist-deep through the water toward the smoke-shrouded, battle-strewn shore. Today the beach attracts tourists with merely the smashed, rusted skeletons of naval craft remaining as mute reminders.

THE PARATROOPERS. First Allied troops to hit German-held France on D-Day were paratroopers. The U.S. IX Troop Carrier Command and the RAF dropped three divisions of these flying ground soldiers behind enemy lines a few minutes after midnight. These were the American 82nd and 101st Airborne Divisions, and the British 6th Division. The American divisions assisted in establishing the Omaha and Utah beaches by disrupting communications and causing as much confusion as possible behind German lines. Their assistance was invaluable when the U.S. First Army hit these beaches. The British landed behind the lines near Ste. Mere Eglise. UPPER LEFT. Somewhere over France a jump master and a crew chief push supplies out to paratroopers who are already doing their work behind German lines. LOWER LEFT. American paratroopers, having landed successfully at St. Marcouf, France, move cautiously into the small village, taking cover and concealment from trees and buildings. UPPER RIGHT. The "boss" looks the situation over on June 8. On the deck of a warship off the coast of northern France General Eisenhower, with General Bradley and Major General Ralph Royce, Deputy Commander of the Ninth Air Force, talk things over and make decisions for future action. LOWER RIGHT. A few hundred yards away, on the same day, American assault troops of the 1st Division, carrying full equipment, move along a cliff on the beach. Vast quantities of equipment, brought ashore from landing craft, lay at the base of this cliff. Except in rare instances—and then only temporarily—did American troops lack equipment.

FIRST MOPPING UP. UPPER. When the artillery and air force had eased up on Isigny, France, these Yanks moved in to wipe it clear of snipers and machine guns. On June 11 they take it easy after their job is done. LOWER. Members of an American landing party help their buddies ashore from a landing craft near Cherbourg on June 12. The craft had been sunk by enemy action. Allied air superiority prevented the dwindling Luftwaffe from doing a great deal of damage to landing operations, though sometimes German planes managed to slip through the defenses and make a quick attack.

ANY CHEWING GUM? In France, as usual, American GIs were big hits with the kids. UPPER. Soldiers of the 747th Tank Battalion, First Army, pass out candy and chewing gum to eager French hands on June 19. It made no difference if these Yanks had to rob their K-rations to do this. They just didn't know how to say no. LOWER. Mulberry and Gooseberry projects, vast landing platforms extending 1,000 yards into the Channel from Omaha Beach, proved instrumental in the transportation of huge quantities of material from landing craft to the continent. Said General Marshall: "The combined planning of British and American staffs, working together as a single team with excellent knowledge of enemy dispositions, resulted in precise execution of an operation so complicated that it almost defies description. Its success must be attributed in great measure to wholehearted Allied cooperation, as well as the stout hearts and fearless courage of the men." All the world had wondered if this venture was going to be successful, and all the Allied world rejoiced that the first week had ended with Allied forces overcoming the resistance of the defenders. The job now was to break out and go on to victory.

CHERBOURG FALLS. After gaining the beachheads, the first major objective of the invasion was capture of Cherbourg so its port facilities could be put to use in building up supplies and manpower. The U.S. VII Corps under Major General J. Lawton Collins cut the Cotentin peninsula in half on June 18. This isolated Cherbourg, and it fell June 27. UPPER. General Collins and his staff look over the port from atop Fort du Roule. LOWER. It took much concentrated offensive action to rid the port of Nazis. Soldiers here take cover as a Nazi pill box goes up in smoke and flames.

"SUPERMEN" GIVE UP. UPPER. German soldiers, most of whom were abandoned by their officers, at Cherbourg, are marched through the streets of the city after its liberation by American forces. This picture was made June 28. LOWER. Frenchmen cheer as American GIs who liberated Cherbourg march through the Place De La Republique. Allied flags were displayed for the first time in four years. Still, out in the harbor area on June 29, desperately-resisting German forces continued to hold out in isolated fortifications. They were soon driven out, and Cherbourg was in Allied hands.

MINED ROADS AGAIN. Though the Germans did leave Rome in great haste, they took time, as usual, to plant plenty of mines and demolitions along the way to make the going rough for the pursuing Allies. In this they succeeded. Often the Fifth Army skirted the heavily-mined roads and took to the hills and byways to make better speed. By July 2 U.S. troops had reached Cecina. On the approaches to Leghorn, the seaport city 15 miles away, they ran into stiff resistance from the Germans, who had had a few days to get ready for the assault. But Leghorn fell on July 19. ABOVE. A soldier, crouching cautiously, watches while others set off mines in one of the main streets leading to Leghorn's harbor.

BREAKTHROUGH IN FRANCE. By mid-July 1944, the Allied schedule in France had gone so far out of whack a terrific "carpet bombing" show was laid on between Periers and St. Lo, July 25th, with 1,883 planes dropping 4,700 tons of bombs in a space 5 miles long and one mile wide. American ground forces were brought up in strength as close as possible to the bomb line, and then the bombers struck. Before the dazed Germans could recover their senses, the First Army had poured through the hole in the dam and the rat race across France was on, with the IX TAC moving along as fast as the 1st Army could gain ground, frequently knocking out obstacles ahead of them so they could move even faster. ABOVE. 8th Air Force B-24s after "Bombs Away!" over Tours, France. Lead bombardier drops smoke marker to show the flight path to the rest of the formation. During the breakthrough phase of action, the Air Force worked in close cooperation with the advancing ground troops. Tactical assistance was rendered whenever possible, and strongly defended points and fortifications were bombed into submission. The enemy's supply and transportation lines were repeatedly blasted to prevent the mounting onrush of reinforcements.

TACTICAL
AIR POWER IN EUROPE

By Lieutenant General Hoyt S. Vandenberg

ON THE morning of August 7, 1944, two weeks after the First American Army had broken out of the Normandy beachhead at St. Lo, the front was visited by Hitler's personal representative, General Warmilont. He was undoubtedly dispatched to find out why the American forces pouring to the south had not been halted. It was a melancholy report he received from Von Kluge, commander of the German armies:

"Whether the enemy can be stopped at this point is still questionable. His air superiority is terrific and smothers almost all our movements. At the same time, every movement of his is prepared and protected by his air force. Our losses in men and equipment are extraordinary. The morale of our troops has suffered heavily under murderous enemy fire. Fresh troops must be brought in ... from somewhere ..."

General Warmilont hesitated to present the news to his chief, but it was undeniable: The "Luftwaffe" was nowhere to be seen, having utterly failed in its greatest crisis. Without it, a mighty "Wehrmacht" was being dissected by an enemy ground force no greater than itself and with considerably less battle experience, but made irresistible by the addition of tactical air power.

Born in combat, tactical air power was introduced to military doctrine in Field Manual 100-20: "Land power and air power are co-equal and interdependent forces; neither is an auxiliary of the other." That statement became a powerhouse punch wielded by air-ground teams.

Before World War II, tactical air was merely a means of augmenting army artillery. Germany's belief in this old concept was a factor in the ultimate defeat of her army. Constant air-ground synchronization in North Africa dictated a new theory of applying power.

Air supremacy was to be the first priority goal, reducing enemy strength until this was accomplished.

The second priority was to isolate the battlefield by cutting troop movements from flank and rear, destroying bridges, roads, vehicles, communications, and supply centers.

Close cooperation with ground forces had third priority. Attack resistance and soften it for advancing ground forces; support infantry; supply armored units with food, ammo, and fuel from the air.

As the campaign in Africa drew to a close in the spring of 1943, plans for the invasion of Europe were taking shape. Headquarters staff of the Ninth Air Force, sent to England, began the feverish task of assembling a tactical air force. There was less than a year to do the job of setting up experimental organizations, gathering and training personnel, exploring the potentialities of a new offensive weapon —radar, and establishing tactics. Above all, planes suitable for new combat tasks had to be obtained and modified, fast B-26 bombers, P-47 fighter-bombers, photo reconnaissance P-38's, and P-51's for tactical reconnaissance.

The first mission of the IX Bomber Command was to hit coastal airfields, where swarms of German fighters rose against our heavy bomber formations when they crossed the Channel. As the bomb damage mounted, they abandoned the attempt to operate fields. The air over the Channel was ours.

The enemy answered with numerous, strong, well concealed flying bomb sites along the Calais-Normandy coasts. They were extremely difficult targets but Allied bombers forced their abandonment and the V-bomb blitz faded out.

Typical of the pre-invasion tasks was the assignment to take low-level pictures of the formidably defended Normandy beaches. In a light, unarmed Lockheed F-5, whose camera was mounted to snap pictures ahead and to the sides of the plane, these intrepid pilots flew their "dicing missions" with their lives in their hands. But they brought back pictures that showed the strong and weak spots in the defenses of the Normandy coast.

Invasion tasks for all Britain-based aircraft were planned in April 1944, calling for maximum air-ground teamwork. On D-Day, when Allied Forces struck at the most vital target, the overland route to Berlin, the "Luftwaffe" failed to appear. The AAF and RAF had made it impossible, the Ninth Air Force alone flying more than 35,000 tactical sorties from May 1st to June 6th. They struck airfields, rail yards, transport, coastal gun positions, communications, and bridges stretching from the Netherlands to the Pyrenees, Just before Allied troops stormed the beaches, medium bombers and fighters flew 100 miles inland to disrupt efforts to bring up reinforcements. Most enemy planes stayed away.

The D-Day air plan was of great complexity and scope. It called for constant fighter cover to protect the invasion convoy, directed by a control ship in the Channel. The Ninth had already destroyed every major bridge over the Seine from Paris to LeHavre to prevent quick shuttle of troops to Normandy. On D-Day, the battle area enclosed by the Seine and Loire was sealed off. The Eighth Air Force bombed all bridges from Blois to Nantes, and the Ninth cut off the Paris-Orleans gap from Beaufency to Nantes. By this latter move, Paris was excluded from the battle area even though it was the transport hub of France.

As our ground forces worked their way inland, every small French field became a German fortress edged with deep drainage ditches and stout hedges. Enemy troops dug in, their camouflage discipline excellent, offering few targets for fighter-bombers. By the middle of July, it was decided to resort to "carpet bombing" to break up the impenetrable German line.

On July 25th at St. Lo, in a space of 7,000 yards long and 250 yards wide, 3,400 tons of HE were dropped by more than 1,500 aircraft of all types. American ground forces were brought up in strength as close as possible to the bomb line before the bombers struck, and immediately after the attack, while the Germans were dazed and unable to coordinate, the First Army had poured through the gap.

A week after the break-through, General Patton's Third Army followed the First through the gap and drove south to the bank of the Loire River. After mopping-up in Brittany, it too turned east and embarked on one of the most remarkable spearheads in modern warfare, teaming up with General Weyland's XIX TAC to protect his flank. In a month General Patton was within 60 miles of Germany.

Weyland's job was three fold. In addition to knocking down bridges on the Loire, he covered Patton's advancing tank columns, and at the same time reduced three ports in Brittany where German garrisons were holding out. The XIX TAC also forced the surrender of 30,000 Germans massed south of Loire, ready to attack Patton.

By the end of August 1944, the Ninth American Army had landed in France, and with it another TAC, the XXIX commanded by General Nugent. Throughout August and into September, the IX, XIX, and XXIX TACs operated at maximum strength. Their flexibility on employment was a valuable capability. When the bomb divisions were forbidden to attack any more bridges, as our rapidly moving ground forces expected to use them, the TACs could be used to force the Germans out into the open. They created vast pockets of enemy troops and vehicles to be crushed between British ground forces and the First American Army, both racing toward Paris. In the Falaise pocket alone, P-47s destroyed about 1,000 vehicles.

The relation of the tactical air commands to ground army became even closer than before as the armies approached the imposing barriers of the Moselle, Meuse, Roer, Oure, Erft and Saar Rivers and the Siegfried Line. Tactical reconnaissance, flown by P-51s, patrolled enemy territory reporting troop and rail movements, and selecting targets for fighter-bombing or strafing. P-38s took daylight pictures of the snow-blanketed enemy and showed details of roads and rivers. A-20s, equipped for night photography, revealed the movements the Germans attempted after dark.

Radar instruments were still in the infancy of development, but by the winter of 1944, they provided for the control and direction of virtually every day or night sortie flown by the IX TAC. They steered fighter planes to targets, vectored them home again, and relieved the strain on pilots by keeping them constantly informed of the presence of other aircraft.

Tactical air appeared to classic advantage during the Germans' Ardennes offensive, the "Battle of the Bulge." Within eight days of launching their attacks, German spearheads were 50 miles into Belgium. Then the weather cleared and hundreds of AAF planes pulverized the airfields, railways, bridges, and communication centers essential to Von Rundstedt's supply lines, and smashed stock he needed to hold his position. In one day, December 24th, tactical aircraft and the Eighth Air Force flew 5,102 tactical sorties. The advancing Allied infantrymen could see the piled up results of TAC operations.

As the advance swept eastward to the Elbe, to Czechoslovakia, and to Austria, the Ninth established airfields east of the Rhine despite opposition and adverse weather. Driven back upon a small number of fields where aircraft were heavily concentrated, the GAF made excellent targets. In the first 18 days of April, our air forces were able to destroy 3,121 planes of all kinds, only 400-500 of them in the air. The "Luftwaffe" had ceased to exist as a fighting force.

As for our air forces, all were now employed tactically. Bombers concentrated on stopping enemy rail traffic. Fighter-bombers devoted themselves to supply air cover for armored columns and the transport planes bearing their fuel.

The Ninth Air Force accomplished its triple mission: It won and maintained air supremacy; it isolated the battlefield, and linked arms with Allied ground armies for combat teamwork. Flexibility and skill in the use of its weapons enabled them to perform varied tasks with conspicuous success, leading to the unconditional surrender of the enemy on 8 May 1945.

Tactical air power has not reached the ultimate in employment. Dependent on the maintenance of a ground army, the services of tactical air become of greater value as new equipment and new tactics are developed. Jet fighter planes and reconnaissance, and round-the-clock bomb groups have been added. To further expand air-ground cooperation, courses have been planned to illustrate tactical air doctrine to AGF officers.

As long as there is a necessity for ground combat troops, there will be a corresponding requirement for tactical air. Its role in the postwar Air Force is large and certain. It will be conducted in the spirit of progress initiated in combat, where tactical air power was born.

Hoyt S. Vandenberg

THE BREAKOUT. The great breakout, for elbow room, came at St. Lo and Avranches on July 25. By that time U.S. forces in the beachhead area totaled 13 Infantry and five Armored Divisions. In addition, the Canadian First Army and the British Second Army were there and ready to go. The breakout was preceded by an unprecedented saturation bombing of enemy lines. More than 2,500 bombers dropped almost 4,500 tons of bombs on a narrow front. UPPER. Vehicles of the 29th Infantry Division in St. Lo July 29. LOWER. Mail being distributed to GIs even in St. Lo.

CRUSHING POWER. The crushing power of this air attack paralyzed the enemy, and blasted the way for rapid penetration of his lines—and the breakout gave Allied commanders an opportunity to deliver mighty blows. UPPER. On July 28 an American infantry patrol passes an unscarred cathedral in the midst of heavy damage in Coutances, France. LOWER. Two days later these American armored and infantry forces pass through another section of Coutances in the new offensive against the Nazis. General Eisenhower directed a vigorous pursuit of the shattered German forces,

MOPPING UP AGAIN. ABOVE. This was a city. Although the town of Vire had been entered by British patrols a week earlier, it had just been fully taken by the Allies when this picture was made August 8. Any movement in the remains of the town caused a rain of fire from Germans who occupied hills overlooking the area. UPPER RIGHT. House to house fighting in St. Malo on August 8 finds these infantrymen drawing beads on snipers who held up occupation for several hours. LOWER RIGHT. American soldiers enjoy hot omelets presented by the French at a village near Champigne, August 8. The town had just been liberated from the Germans after an occupation of several years.

"SWEATING IT OUT." As this picture was taken, a few days before the invasion of Southern France, thousands of troops of the 3rd Division await their turn to board nearby landing craft for the big operation. Other members of the Allied command watch the operations from a high wall overlooking an Italian port. The area chosen for the landings in Southern France was situated south of the famous pre-war resort area of Nice, Cap d'Antibes and Cannes. At only one point was German resistance so heavy that the landing forces could not be disembarked. Veterans of the Anzio landings, which had also been initially easy but were followed by fierce German counter-attacks, waited for the Nazis to open up. Instead, the advance groups pushed on virtually unmolested as far as 30 miles inland, striking through the valleys and foothills to the Maritime Alps. Three days later, 7,000 German prisoners, including a general and his staff, had been captured, against a total of 300 Allied casualties. The weakness of the German opposition was a surprise to the Allied command, headed by General Sir Henry Maitland Wilson, Supreme Allied Commander in the Mediterranean. The German High Command, at least, must have been cognizant of the operation for King George VI, Prime Minister Winston Churchill, U.S. Secretary of the Navy Forrestal, and Under-Secretary of War Robert P. Patterson had all recently visited Italy, and more than 800 ships had been assembled in the area. Nevertheless, resistance by the foe was negligible.

AIRBORNE INVASION OF SOUTHERN FRANCE. For several weeks prior to D-Day, the Allies had followed the same tactics which preceded the Normandy landings. Bombers smashed bridges and road junctions surrounding the landing area until it was virtually isolated, repeating their work elsewhere to avoid giving away the exact spot of the attack. Every railroad bridge across the Rhone below Valence was knocked out. Then, just before the assault, the huge Allied armada moved close to shore points and shelled the more important defense installations. Airborne troops were dropped behind beaches to secure important road junctions and bridges. Then the landings began. As Prime Minister Winston Churchill watched the operation from the bridge of a British destroyer, the beaches were inundated with men, vehicles and tanks. In this picture, paratroopers fill the sky over Southern France after the 12th USAAF troop carrier air division's Douglas C-47's had carried the men and supplies to dropping zones over the new beachhead located in the vicinity of Nice.

SOUTHERN FRANCE ASSAULT FORMS UP. Originally planned to coincide with the invasion of Normandy, the Southern France operation was delayed in order to assemble a larger striking force and to include some of the ships that had taken part in operation "Neptune." The invasion itself was one of the worst kept secrets of the war; shoeshine boys in Naples could, and did, discuss the place and approxi-mate date of the coming attack. In a four-pronged assault designed to capture important southern French ports, convoys made up in far-flung ports. LST's sailed from Naples, LCI's, LCT's from Corsica. UPPER. Line after line of vehicles in Naples await loading. LOWER. LST's, packed with Army equipment, loading for the invasion in Naples harbor as soldiers shuttle through the bow doors.

GERMAN RESISTANCE WEAK. German resistance in Southern France was so unexpectedly weak that troops ashore by the end of D-Day were already a day ahead of schedule. One German air attack occurred the evening of D-Day, destroying an LST, but that was all. In addition to U.S. troops, 300,000 French troops under General de Lattre de Tassigny took part in the campaign. More difficult objectives, however, were the ports of Toulon and Marseille which were defended by heavy German artillery. UPPER. Victorious American troops head into Marseille Harbor in an LCVP. Fort St. Jean lies directly ahead. LOWER. Troops and equipment pour ashore from an LST onto a beach where once gay vacationers sunned themselves in the halcyon days before the European continent became a world battlefield.

THE BEAUTIFUL CITY. There was much rejoicing all over the Allied world when Paris fell into Allied hands August 25. The elation of General Le Clerc (upper left), holding cane, must have surpassed all others. He was commanding general of the 2nd French Armored Division, and his tanks, shown rolling in here August 25, were the first Allied units to reach the capital. LOWER LEFT. This is a long shot of Paris on the day of her liberation. While this picture was being made American and French forces, aided by the Free French and Maquis inside the city, were battling the remaining Germans for the capital. UPPER RIGHT. American GIs had liberated many a town from Tunisia to Rome, but there was never a welcome to equal the one they got from the French when they rolled into Paris from the victories in Normandy. The crowds went wild, and the GIs loved it. Language was no barrier as the French threw flowers and kisses. Here happy French children and adults cheer a truckload of Yanks as they enter the city by truck August 25. LOWER RIGHT. The fun is spoiled here temporarily. A whole square full of Parisians who had been celebrating the entry of Allied troops scatter for cover as a sniper—the inevitable sniper — fires into them from a building across the street. And this was a day after the liberation! Though the Germans had surrendered the city and were hiking it for their own country, small bands of snipers still remained. By the time of Paris' liberation, General Marshall said the enemy had suffered at least 400,000 casualties, of which more than 200,000 were prisoners of war. Those units that had escaped destruction left behind countless tons of materiel.

VICTORY PARADE. Even though the happy Parisians were impressed with what they saw of America's might on the day of liberation, they had a greater thrill coming a few days later when more troops and vehicles rolled in. ABOVE. Parisians line the famous Champs Elysees on August 29 to cheer as row after row of American vehicles, demonstrating U.S. mechanized might, parade toward the Arc de Triomphe. UPPER RIGHT. A close view of the 28th Infantry Division on the Champs Elysees during the victory parade. Meanwhile, in the south of France, other operations were underway. On August 15 the U.S. Seventh Army under Lieutenant General Alexander M. Patch, had landed at several points around Cannes, Toulon and Marseille. The aim was to strike up the Rhone Valley. LOWER RIGHT. A priest of Notre Dame, in Marseille, greets French soldiers late in August on the debris-littered steps of the church.

FROM PISA TO ARNO. The capture of Leghorn was followed by hard fighting for the famed Italian city of Pisa. Many a GI got a look at the "Leaning Tower," built in 1174. But that was only incidental to the task ahead, for beyond Pisa lay the Arno, and beyond that the German-held Gothic Line. For the push across the Arno and Gothic Line, an offensive was launched early in the fall, 1944, with partial success. The line was actually breached when the key positions at the Giogo Pass were captured. However, bad weather, coupled with a shortage of men and materiel, halted the operations in the mountains of Bologna until the spring of 1945. ABOVE. Yank troops head toward the "Leaning Tower" of Pisa.

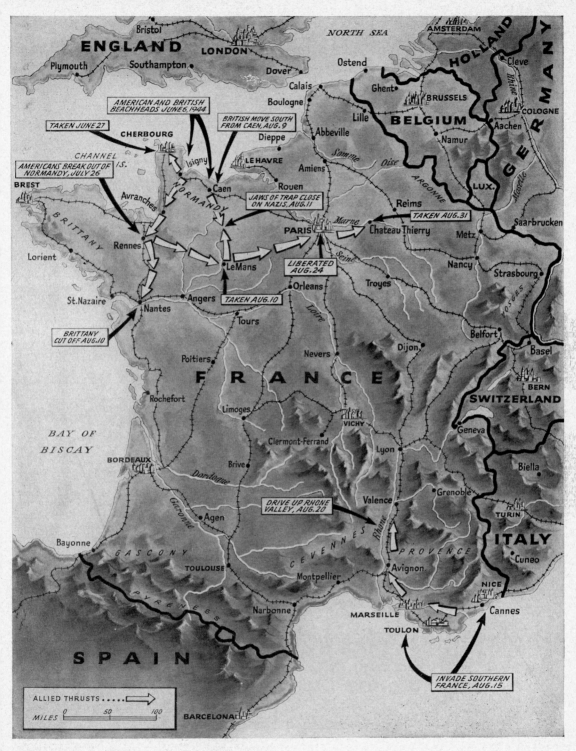

STORY OF THE LIBERATION. The trail of white arrows on the map (above), marks German defeats in France. After landing on the shores of Normandy, American and British troops were stopped for weeks. On July 26, the Americans broke out below Avranches, while on August 9, the British pushed through at Caen. The decisive factor in the Battle for France was the pocketing of German armies in Normandy. The sweep to the east was then possible.

THE CHASE. After Paris, the Germans headed for the protection of the Siegfried Line, with the Allies in hot pursuit.
Allied forces broke out of the Seine bridgeheads, and were
soon to overrun northern France, Luxembourg, Belgium and
southern Holland. UPPER. A wounded Yank in foreground,
hit by a Nazi machine gun slug from across Moselle River
September 5. He was carried to safety while bullets whizzed
overhead. LOWER. American armor fans out near Gelin,
Belgium, to blast at trapped German infantry. The Germans
were still retreating slowly at this stage of the campaign.

INTO BELGIUM. On the north of the Allied front, the American First Army crossed the Belgian border on September 2. Six days later it captured Liege, crossed Luxembourg, and entered German territory September 11. UPPER. As scattered townspeople wave them on, troops with jeeps and half tracks advance through Namur, Belgium, on September 5. LOWER. In Libin, Belgium, on September 7, men of the 8th Regiment, 4th Infantry Division, attempt to move forward, but are pinned down temporarily by German small arms fire. GIs seek cover behind road signs and return fire.

BATTLE IN BELGIUM. The Germans put up a stout defense against the First Army's drive into Belgium, but they could not halt it. UPPER. Here a 155 mm "Long Tom" mounted on a Sherman tank chassis sends a shell into German positions across the Moselle River in Belgium. As the gunner at left yanks the firing lanyard the soldier in foreground crouches and holds his ears to avoid concussion. Note smoke ring flaring out of the muzzle. LOWER. Taken on September 8, 1944, in Liege, Belgium. A Yank infantryman pokes the muzzle of his rifle around a street corner to take a shot at a German sniper hidden in the building at the end of the street. Up to this point in the war, the Allies were jubilant over their success in breaching the Normandy beaches, driving across France and moving into Germany itself. General Eisenhower had declared that the offensive was nearly a week ahead of schedule, and soon he was to send a message to the German people declaring that German militarism was to be eradicated completely. Nor was this to be empty talk. The Allies were prepared for just this task.

SLUGGER FOR TACTICAL AIR FORCES. Although designed as a high altitude fighter with 18-cylinder air-cooled radial engine with turbo-supercharger for it to "breathe" in the high thin air, the Republic P-47 Thunderbolt turned out to be one of the most powerful low-level fighter-bombers on either side during the last two years of the war. With its eight .50-cal. machine guns (a total of 6,400 rounds per minute) plus a bomb under each wing, as shown, the P-47 was one of the most lethal and most effective weapons on the battlefield, as the enemy learned.

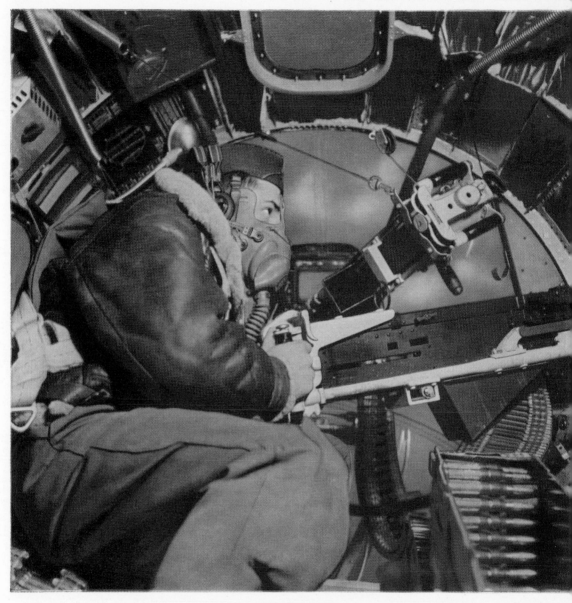

NO REST FOR THE BOMBARDIER. En route to the home base after bombing enemy installations with the aid of his Norden bombsight, the bombardier has to be on the alert for enemy "bandits" as he mans the nose gun of his B-17. The bombardier was the key man of the heavy bomber crew, was thoroughly trained to make the most of his job, including not only bombardment techniques, but navigation and aerial gunnery as well. In later models of the B-17 (the G model) the nose gun was done away with entirely, its place being taken by the Bendix remote-controlled chin turret, with computing gun-sight and electronic aiming of .50-cal. guns in the turret. This in turn was but a shadow that forecast the ingenious remote-controlled armament system developed by General Electric for the B-29. However, in the first couple of years of the war, and in some theaters all through it, the gunners used to swing their guns by hand, and they downed plenty of enemy fighters, too.

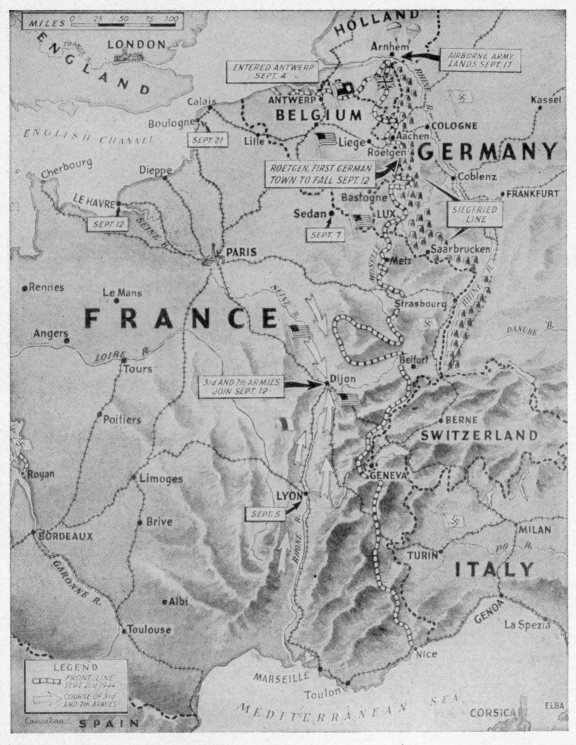

FIRST HAMMERBLOWS AT GERMANY. With the speedy drive through France to the borders of the Reich, the battle of France was ended and final operations for the defeat of Germany were begun. In many places the Sieg-fried Line had been breached and the Allies made a quick and daring bid to run the northern end of the line with air-borne troops. This was unsuccessful and many weeks were required to break through the formidable Westwall defenses.

NAZIS FEEL ALLIED PINCH. After the Allied armies had battered the "Wehrmacht" out of France, they turned the guns of the Maginot Line (upper) around against the retreating Germans, and assaulted the famed Siegfried Line. LOWER. Yanks and their bulldozer tanks easily pass through this break in the Westwall situated near Roetgen, Germany.

THE FORCES MEET. The first meeting of American troops of General Patton's Third Army and General Patch's Seventh Army took place on September 13 at Autun, France. A French driver whose native group had landed near Toulon shakes hands with members of Combat Command B of the Third Army's 6th Armored Division in a street of the city. The meeting was symbolic in that it was one of those junctures that presaged the doom of the Nazi armies.

BOMBS PIERCE BREST'S HARD SHELL. The great port and
U-boat base of Brest was besieged for 46 days before surrendering to American troops on September 21, 1944. The
port was attacked by land and air. Concentrated bombing
aided materially in the surrender. ABOVE. Eighth Air Force
planes blast a small quay of the Brest peninsula.

A REAL BEATING. This is Brest as it appeared on the day the Ninth Army took it. The destruction is reminiscent of Cassino, in Italy. Brest took a real beating, and hardly a building was left unscathed. In this view (upper) dry dock installations are visible in background. Notice that few of the buildings have roofs left over them. LOWER. Two Army first aid men search for injured through what had been a street in Brest. Whenever they had a chance the Germans demolished port facilities as much as possible to prevent their immediate re-use by the Allies.

FROM D-DAY TO THE ARDENNES

By General Omar N. Bradley

EARLY on the morning of 6 June 1944, combined British-American forces under the supreme command of General Dwight D. Eisenhower assaulted the German-fortified Normandy coast of France.

Operation OVERLORD, as the invasion plan was called, had been in preparation more than two years, and represented the culmination of Allied hopes to return to the European continent and destroy the German armies in the west.

First troops to reach French soil were the American 82nd and 101st Airborne Divisions, and the British 6th Airborne Division. All were dropped in vital areas in the rear of German coastal defenses shortly after midnight of 6 June. Aerial bombardment began at about 0300, and three hours later Naval escorts, including battleships, cruisers, and destroyers, joined the battle.

Behind this screen of fire landing craft swarmed the beaches; the first waves of assault infantry and tanks landed at 0630. Elements of the First U.S. Army—under my command—and the Second British Army climbed ashore west of the Orne River and on the east of the Cotentin peninsula. With airborne assistance the British quickly won a beachhead and pushed inland to the approaches of Bayeux and Caen. In the center of the U.S. V Corps, under Major General (now Lieutenant General) Leonard T. Gerow, met unexpected enemy strength, but seized a foothold. On the right the U.S. VII Corps, under Major General (now General) J. Lawton Collins, quickly secured a beachhead on the east coast of the Cotentin.

Despite fierce resistance the landings were merged into a secure beachhead within a week, and limited advances were made in all areas. Men and supplies were hurried ashore. An average of 37,500 men landed each day, and in the first five days 16 Allied divisions were concentrated in France.

Our first major objective was won after the VII Corps cut the Cotentin peninsula on 18 June, and went on to capture the port of Cherbourg nine days later. This port was to prove vital for many months in building up and maintaining our forces.

During the next 30 days United States forces fought through the tenaciously-held hedgerow country of Normandy. The object was to gain elbow room and secure a lodgement for building up forces large enough to launch decisive blows. These hedgerows, three to five feet high, and covered by dense growth, afforded the enemy an excellent natural protection which he capitalized. The first big Allied drive came with the breakout at St. Lo. On 25 July, after an unprecedented saturation bombing of enemy lines, the First U.S. Army pierced German defenses and reached Granville five days later. On 1 August, while the First Canadian and Second British Armies pushed south and west, the Third U.S. Army, under Lieutenant General George S. Patton, Jr., became operational and joined the First U.S. Army under Lieutenant General Courtney H. Hodges. These armies were formed into the 12th Army Group under my command.

While the First Army moved toward Mortain the Third Army struck southward, from Avranches, poured troops and supplies through the gap there, and then struck south, east, and west.

With the enemy's left flank crumbling, destruction of the German Seventh Army west of the Seine became a distinct possibility. With General Eisenhower's approval I took steps to exploit the situation by directing the Third Army to make its major effort eastward toward the Laval-Le-Mans-Chartres area, leaving only minimum forces to clear Brittany.

On August 7 the Germans made a desperate attempt to cut the Avranches corridor at Mortain and isolate the Third Army, but they failed after three days of bitter fighting. Soon large elements of the Third Army were completely in the rear of the Germans, and the attack was directed northward toward Alencon in conjunction with a 21st Army Group attack toward Falaise. Our aim was encirclement of the enemy. Before this encirclement was completed by a meeting of U.S. and Canadian troops at Chambois on 19 August, considerable of the enemy's forces managed to escape, but his losses in killed and captured totaled 70,000.

Continuing eastward, the Third Army captured Orleans, Chartres, and Dreux, and crossed the Seine near Melum south of Paris on 24 August. The next day Paris was liberated by the First Army. With exception of the seizure of Brest, St. Nazaire, and Lorient, which were under attack or being contained, the objective of Operation OVERLORD was achieved just 80 days after the invasion.

Meanwhile, the Seventh U.S. Army, under Lieutenant General Alexander M. Patch, with elements of the First French Army attached, had assaulted the southern coast of France on 15 August between Cannes and Toulon, and advanced rapidly up the Rhone Valley. Success of this drive and our victory in the Falaise-Argentan pocket, afforded an opportunity to send strong forces to the Ruhr industrial area, and to the Saar.

Allied forces crossed the Seine, and between 26 and 30 September overran northern France,

Luxembourg, Belgium and southern Holland. The Third Army had crossed the Meuse and pushed rapidly to the Moselle. By 11 September the First Army had penetrated the Siegfried Line near Aachen, and on the same day elements of the Third Army contacted the Seventh Army and closed the escape route for German forces remaining between the Rhone and Loire rivers. Thus the Allies had formed a continuous front from Switzerland to the North Sea.

After reaching the Siegfried Line in the north, and the Moselle River in the south, the Allied drive lost its momentum. The advance of more than 400 miles in a month and a half had left us with over-extended supply lines. Too, our offensive was blunted by the heavily-fortified defense belt the enemy had had time to man. In addition, we had spread out on a front several times that held in the beachhead.

By November plans were made for resumption of a major offensive to carry us across the Rhine.

Preceded by the heaviest close support air bombardment that had yet been delivered, this attack was launched on 16 November north of the Ardennes by the First and Ninth Armies. The Ninth, under Lieutenant General William H. Simpson, had by that time been deployed on the left of the First Army. Progress was slow, but by 3 December the Ninth had reached the Roer River, and on the 13th the First was launching an attack to seize the Schmidt dams which controlled the flooding of the Roer Valley.

In the south, a Third Army attack was more successful. By 22 November it had captured Metz, and in early December penetrated the Siegfried defenses in the vicinity of Saarlautern. Still farther south the Sixth Army Group, which had attacked on 13 November, was having success. The First French Army was breaching the Belfort Gap and reaching the Rhine, while the Seventh Army had broken through the Saverne Gap, cleared Strasbourg, and penetrated the Siegfried Line near Wisembourg.

By mid-December—except for a pocket at Colmar—Allied forces had closed to the Rhine from Basle to the German border and were driving into Germany on a wide front. Extending this front northward, the Third Army was closing to the Siegfried Line as far north as Luxembourg. The First Army had reached the Roer in the north, held the Our River sector from south of Malmedy to the border of Luxembourg, and was advancing slowly through the Hurtgen Forest toward the Roer dams. The Ninth Army had reached the Roer northeast of Aachen.

This was the disposition of our forces when the enemy, on orders from Hitler, launched the offensive to be known as The Battle of the Bulge.

Omar N Bradley

THEIR ULTIMATUM GOES UNANSWERED. More than a week of savage street fighting gave the German city of Aachen to the American First Army on October 21. Ten days earlier, a "surrender or die" ultimatum to the German garrison was rejected and the attack resumed with renewed force. ABOVE. Three United States envoys pick their way through rubble to present the ultimatum to the Germans.

UPPER RIGHT. Elements of the 2nd Battalion, 26th Infantry, advance toward an intersection in the city on October 17. LOWER RIGHT. Aided by armor, Yanks of Company M, 26th Infantry, move up through pock-marked streets to engage the enemy in Aachen in an attempt to force the terms of the surrender. Aachen was the first large German town to be taken by the Allies in World War II.

EXTENDING LINES. After the Allies had reached the Siegfried Line in the north and the Moselle River in the south—and after the Seventh and Third Armies had made contact—the Germans were faced with a homogeneous front from Switzerland to the North Sea. In October the Allied drive had lost some of its momentum. The forces had advanced more than 400 miles in about six weeks, and this left over-extended supply lines. Also, the Germans had had time to man their fortified defense belt, and this slowed down the offensive. For about six weeks in the fall of 1944, therefore, there was relative inactivity all along the front. This period was used to extend and develop supply lines, build up reserves, and in general to get ready for smashing across the Roer and Rhine Rivers. UPPER. In addition to this movement and build-up, there was some fighting, as many a GI would testify. Here on November 10, Company L, 142nd Infantry Regiment, marches from front lines during a snow storm in the Langefosse area of France. LOWER. These hungry infantrymen of the Seventh Army waste no time when they hear the call "seconds on cake."

PORT OF Le HAVRE. The great French port city of Le Havre had fallen before the Allied advance on September 11. The Germans had demolished it to such an extent that it could not be used to advantage for nearly a month. But, unlike Brest, which was damaged almost beyond repair, tonnage began coming in at Le Havre on October 9. Many of the troops and much of the equipment that was to be used in the Allied advance across the Rhine and into the heart of Germany came in through this port. UPPER. Though many of the docks were repaired by time this picture was made November 15, an LST, which scorned dock facilities, goes directly onto the beach at Le Havre to unload Army troops. LOWER. Limited docking facilities made it impossible for all the ships arriving at Le Havre to tie up. So many of them dropped anchor as close to shore as possible, and supplies were carried ashore in invasion style. These U.S. Army "ducks," operating from ship to shore, are loaded with gasoline drums. The Liberty ship in background is one of hundreds of its type that brought the goods of war from the farms and factories of the United States.

THE NOVEMBER OFFENSIVE. In mid-November, when General Eisenhower, with 3,000,000 troops on the continent, launched his winter offensive, some of the worst weather Europe had seen for years hampered movement. Nevertheless, the assault was continued with the aim of putting troops in position to cross the Rhine. Resistance was bitter, the Siegfried Line defenses were formidable, and the weather was awful. Under such conditions Allied divisions paid heavily for every foot of ground they took from the fanatical Nazis—but they took it. Some of the war's bloodiest fighting occurred east of Aachen, where the U.S. First Army moved through Hurtgen Forest, taking heavy casualties and inflicting even greater losses on the Germans. UPPER. With rifles ready troops of Company E, 110th Infantry, 28th Divisions, push through a maze of trees in the forest November 2. LOWER. American tanks of the 803rd Battalion, 3rd Armored Division, take a hairpin curve on a muddy road in the forest November 18. Elsewhere, the offensive was also in full swing. The U.S. Ninth Army was fighting toward the Roer River, and the British Second Army was clearing the west bank of the Meuse.

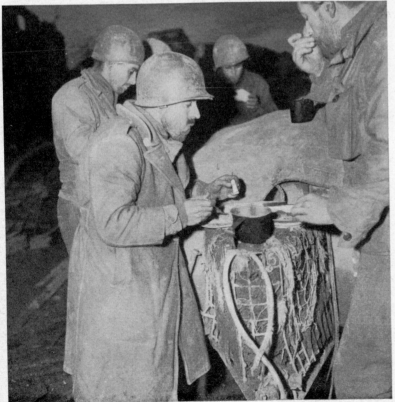

HURTGEN ADVANCE. UPPER. This action in Hurtgen Forest occurred November 26. While smoke from a first volley still clings to the ground, Battery A, 18th Field Artillery Battalion, reloads rocket launchers for a second try at Germans across the way, northwest of Kleinhau. LOWER. The china platters seem out of place as Yank infantrymen eat their first hot meal after 15 days of siege of the town of Hurtgen. The soldiers, worn out from the ordeal they have gone through, belong to Company I, 121st Regiment of the 8th Infantry Division. General Eisenhower wrote of this offensive: "There can be no question of the value of our present operations. The German is throwing into the line some divisions with only six weeks training, a fact that contributes materially to his high casualty rate . . . Our problem is to continue our attacks as long as the results achieved are so much in our favor, while at the same time preparing for a full-out heavy offensive when weather conditions become favorable, assuming the enemy holds out. Unless some trouble develops within Germany . . . he should be able to maintain a strong defensive front for some time. . . ." This belief was correct as later events proved.

AN OLD WAR TECHNIQUE MODERNIZED. Reminiscent of
the days when skill in tree to tree fighting won small tribal
wars, these 20th Century warriors pursue the grim business of
hunting down and killing their foe in the wooded battle-

fields of the Western Front. The scene is dramatically depicted here as two Yanks advance while a companion covers
them with a tommygun. A slain Nazi lies in the foreground.
There are two alternatives . . . kill or be killed.

SHERMAN WAS RIGHT. If the fighting in Hurtgen was tough on the American GI, it was even tougher on his counterpart in Hitler's armies. They were on the losing end of a rough deal. UPPER. These battle-weary Nazis were the last to surrender in the battle of Hurtgen Forest. Note the appearance of fatigue on the soldier at right, and the extreme youth of the Nazi on the left. As General Eisenhower had said, Hitler was by now scraping the bottom of his barrel and sending troops into the line with very little training or preparation. These Germans were captured December 12 by Company I, 2nd Battalion of the 39th Regiment. LOWER. Advance troops of the 79th Infantry Division move through Bischwiller, Germany, on December 9. An American soldier lies dead in the foreground. By December 3 the U.S. Ninth Army under Lieutenant General William H. Simpson had reached the Roer River, and on the 13th the First Army was launching an attack to seize the Schmidt Dams which controlled the flooding of the Roer Valley. These dams caused considerable anxiety on the part of General Bradley. By blowing them up the Germans could send a sudden rush of water down the valley and bog operations.

CLOSING IN. By the middle of December, 1944, the Allies were closing in on the Germans from almost all directions. At the same time, Russian forces were smashing westward and were destined soon to meet the Allies. Except for a pocket at Colmar, Allied forces had closed to the Rhine from Basel to the German border. By now Hitler must have known the jig was about up, for his foe was driving into Germany proper on a wide front. In the north the Third Army was closing to the Siegfried Line even to Luxembourg. The First Army had reached the Roer and was advancing slowly through the Hurtgen Forest toward its dams. The Ninth was at the Roer northeast of Aachen. In spite of the weather, floods, stiff resistance and muddy ground, great gains had been made, and Allied commanders were continuing their plans for the drive that would carry them across the Rhine. Regroupings for this task were in progress when the Ardennes offensive of the Germans began. UPPER. Troops of First Army move through snow-covered Krinkelter woods in Belgium December 13. LOWER. Elements of a Seventh Army battalion take a rest at entrance and in pit of a Maginot Line fort near Climbach, France, December 15.

THE BATTLE OF THE BULGE

By Major General Anthony C. McAuliffe

EARLY on the morning of 16 December 1944 heavy enemy shelling and attacks by German infantry, in battalion and company strength, signaled the opening of a great German counteroffensive on the Ardennes sector of the northern Allied front.

The savage action that followed is now known to millions of Americans as the "Battle of the Bulge."

The sector chosen by Hitler for this last desperate attempt to seize the initiative from the victorious Allies and to revive the fading prestige of the Third Reich was held by one newly-arrived division and two depleted and battle-worn divisions. These were thinly deployed over an extended front.

General Eisenhower had taken a calculated risk in this disposition of weak forces along the 75-mile front between Trier and Monschau because he wished to throw the strongest possible weight into the battles in the Aachen sector and along the Saar-Wissembourg front in the south. In addition, the Ardennes terrain was difficult, especially during the winter, and there were no large depots or important strategic objectives in this area.

During the earlier lull in activity on the Roer front the Germans had secretly massed a large force behind the Our River, facing the Ardennes. When fully committed in the Ardennes counteroffensive, this force would consist of the Fifth and Sixth Panzer Armies, and the Seventh Army; the whole totaling some 14 infantry and 10 panzer or panzer grenadier divisions. The strategic employment of this force, which had been personally planned by Hitler, aimed at driving a wedge between the British and American forces in the north and the American and French forces in the south by a blitz thrust to the Meuse River in the Liege-Namur area. Once having seized Liege, which was the chief communication center for the American 12th Army Group, the enemy intended to drive on to the great port of Antwerp, and by its capture render the supply situation of the Allied armies in the north untenable. Finally, Hitler hoped to weaken the Allied will to continue the offensive which had progressed unremittingly from the Normandy beaches to the Siegfried Line.

On 16 and 17 December the German counteroffensive grew in intensity. The enemy struck with speed and determination all along the American front from Echternach to Kronenburg. Armored spearheads knifed into and around the weak American formations, isolating defending units and disrupting communications. Strong columns of enemy infantry and self-propelled artillery followed close on the heels of the tanks, expanding the holes in the American lines and attacking isolated units. The weather, in the first days, favored Hitler. The ground was frozen and permitted the rapid movement of the German panzer tanks. The skies were heavily overcast, and, for the first time since the beginning of the invasion, offered the German ground troops freedom from air attack.

As early as 16 December General Eisenhower had sensed that this new activity, in what had been a quiet sector, was more than merely a series of local counterattacks. On that date he instructed General Bradley to move the 10th Armored Division from the south and the 7th Armored Division from the north against the flanks of the inrushing German attack. At the same time he ordered the 101st and 82nd Airborne Divisions forward from their positions in SHAEF reserve.

During the first 48 hours of the attack the 4th, 28th, and 106th Infantry Divisions, and the 9th Armored Division, had appreciably blunted the initial break-through in the First Army area, but at great cost to themselves. On 18 and 19 December the armored divisions, which had been rushed forward from the Third and Ninth Armies, and the two airborne divisions, now fighting as ground troops, were engaged in the battle area.

In the absence of Major General Maxwell D. Taylor, I was in temporary command of the 101st Airborne Division. This Division—fortunately reinforced by Combat Command B, 10th Armored Division; the 705th Tank Destroyer Battalion and some artillery—was directly in the path of the German attack. Its task was to hold the important road center at Bastogne.

Here, on 22 December, when the Division was encircled by enemy forces, the Germans requested that the besieged garrison surrender. And it was here, on the same day, that we gave them the answer—"Nuts!" The Germans initially could not translate this reply, but they soon understood that the Division had no intention of surrendering.

Fortunately, though completely surrounded and attacked by many times its own numbers, the Bastogne garrison continued to hold this important position, and thus impeded the German drive toward the Meuse.

Meanwhile, General Eisenhower had acted to strip the rest of the Allied front and bring additional divisions into the Ardennes battleground. In the south, General Devers was ordered to extend his left and thus relieve as many of General Patton's Third Army divisions as possible, weakening his own lines and even giving ground if that was necessary. The Third Army was instructed to give up its attack at the Saar and thus free the forces necessary for a counterattack against the enemy's southern flank. North of the Bulge, Marshal Montgomery collected a British corps as a reserve in the Brussels area. General Hodge's First Army assembled an American Corps under General Collins for use as a counterattack force, and at the same time shored up the northern shoulder of the German penetration. The last Theater Reserves, the 17th Airborne Division and the 11th Armored Division, were brought up to the Meuse River to meet, if necessary, the German columns still on the march toward the west.

On 22 December the Third Army forces were in position and launched the initial large scale counterattack against the Germans' southern flank, striking from the vicinity of Arlon toward encircled Bastogne. Providentially, or so it seemed to the American soldiers, the skies cleared on 23 December and remained clear for five days. The Air Forces at once intervened, pounding the German columns and supply dumps silhouetted against the snow. The losses inflicted on the enemy were enormous, and this Allied air effort contributed greatly to the final defeat of Hitler's aspirations in the Bulge.

The Third Army attack went slowly in its initial stages against strong opposition. On the northern shoulder, after tenacious fighting, the Americans lost the St. Vith position, which had stuck like a thorn in the German flank. By the close of 26 December, the three German armies had reached the highwater mark of the counteroffensive, but the German detachments farthest westward still were short of the Meuse River line. That same night the lead tanks of the Fourth Armored Division rolled into Bastogne; they opened a corridor from the south along which reinforcements and supplies could reach the hard-fighting garrison.

All enemy attempts to sever this corridor were repulsed, and the Allies commenced to push in the nose and southern flank of the Bulge. The Third Army attack to drive obliquely across the salient, in the direction of St. Vith, moved steadily but slowly. At the close of December a regrouping in the north, carried out under Marshal Montgomery's direction, brought British reinforcements opposite the tip of the German tongue and permitted the creation of a counterattack force in the First Army area. On 3 January 1945, General Hodge's troops began a counterattack from the north, driving toward Houffalize to meet the Third Army forces moving up from the south. Slowly the First and Third armies converged, supported by heavy artillery fire and massed air attacks. But the broken terrain, the weather, and desperate delaying actions by the enemy, combined to hold the jaws of the trap open for several days. Finally, on 16 January, Hodges and Patton joined forces at Houffalize, flattening the Bulge still more. Eight days later St. Vith was retaken. The salient was collapsing rapidly, although the enemy still formed a continuous front as they retreated, and this was true despite brutal punishment dealt out by the fighter-bombers.

At the close of January all of the ground lost during the German counteroffensive had been regained. The Battle of the Bulge was ended and the Allies prepared to drive through the Siegfried Line and across the Rhine River.

a. c. mcAuliffe.

"WEHRMACHT'S" LAST BLOW. Early on the morning of December 16, 1944, Field Marshal von Rundstedt, acting on direct orders from Adolph Hitler, began operations that have since become known the world over as the Battle of the Bulge. The Marshal was in command of 20 divisions facing the invading Allies on the German frontier, and he used all of them in this offensive that was destined to be the last blow of the once-mighty "Wehrmacht." Despite a shortage of troops and supplies for the big job General Eisenhower and his commanders and troops had undertaken—a drive to the Rhine and into the heart of Germany—plans to keep up the offensive were in operation. Thus the Allies were compelled to hold some sections of the front with relatively weak forces so that strength could be gathered at points of attack. For about 75 miles between Monschau and Trier the General could assign only four divisions of the First Army, or else sacrifice an effort to bring about a decision elsewhere. It was here that von Rundstedt struck, and that the Germans made their last desperate effort to stave off disaster. ABOVE. This picture, from a captured German film, shows a Nazi soldier examining a litter of abandoned Yank ration boxes and uniforms December 17. UPPER RIGHT. Four dead American soldiers on the western front. LOWER RIGHT. Captured German film shows U.S. captives under guard.

ATROCITIES. The Germans failed to play fair in their surprise offensive in the Ardennes. On the second day of the assault a group of U.S. troops was forced to surrender. After this act the Nazis shot them down in cold blood in the vicinity of Five Points, near Malmedy, Belgium, and their bodies were left where they had fallen in the snow. ABOVE. One of them lies face down in a snow bank, tagged by troops who recaptured the area. UPPER RIGHT. Near Malmedy on December 17 a GI puts identification tags on still more of these victims. LOWER RIGHT. A truck load of these men who were shot after their surrender is unloaded at Malmedy. This was one of the worst atrocities of the war in Europe.

MALMEDY RETAKEN. The Germans' counter offensive overran Malmedy and sent sharp, knife-like armor into Allied lines along other sections of the front. Reinforcements were sent hurriedly into danger areas. These included the 101st and 82nd Airborne Divisions. No sooner had the 101st taken up position at Bastogne when this city was isolated by the Nazi advance, and an epic defense was made there. UPPER. On December 27 members of the 4th Armored Division fire in their advance to relieve the pressure on Bastogne. LOWER. A PX sign left behind in Malmedy.

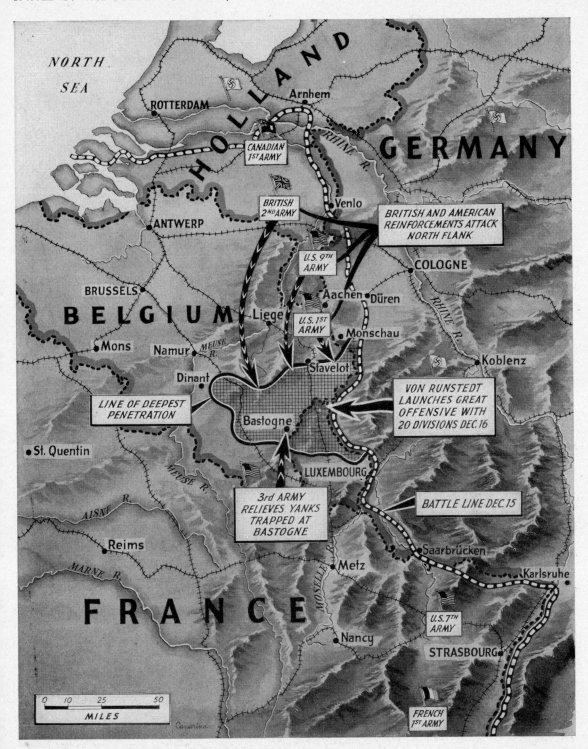

VON RUNDSTEDT COUNTER-ATTACKS. The one great, desperate effort of the German High Command to stem and turn the tide of Allied victories in Europe was their massive counter-attack against the U.S. First Army's lines in Belgium and Luxembourg. Von Rundstedt's divisions (20 in all) overran the shaded areas on the map (above) within a few days, whereupon the Allies brought them up short, struck at their flanks, ripped them from the air, and finally put them to rout.

OPERATION GRIEF. The Germans called their Ardennes offensive "Operation 'Greif'." It was aptly named, because that is what it came to. Two days before Christmas the weather, which had been terrible, and which favored the aggressor, cleared up and the Allied tactical air forces were able to go to work on the armor and supply columns of the enemy. The day after Christmas the 4th Armored Division relieved encircled Bastogne. The crisis was passed by now, and the German salient was being assaulted from the north, west and south. But in the 50-mile penetration into Allied lines there had been fierce fighting—some of the hardest of the entire war. UPPER. On December 19 infantrymen of the 71st Infantry Regiment investigate battle-scarred Sinesshoff Fortress on the Maginot Line near Bitche, France. U.S. troops captured the fort after five days of repeated aerial and artillery bombardment. LOWER. Covered by a buddy in the background a soldier of the 82nd Airborne Division goes out on a one-man sortie near Bra, Belgium, on December 24. After Christmas and the advent of good weather, the Nazi was never able to shake loose the valiant Allied units fighting desperately to hold and defeat him.

AN AERIAL DOG FIGHT. UPPER. This remarkable picture was made on Christmas Day, 1944, in Germany while the Battle of the Bulge was raging in Belgium. Near Puffendorf, Germany, three American GIs are silhouetted against a section of sky almost completely covered with vapor trails left by struggling Allied and German fighter planes. These GIs are patiently waiting to fire on any enemy plane that sweeps low on a strafing operation. **LOWER.** Several men of the 11th Infantry, 5th Division, are wearing white as camouflage while advancing through an orchard in Luxembourg.

ZERO WEATHER. The fighting to reduce the Bulge salient was in some of the worst weather Europe had had in years. Rain, snow and ice hampered operations, and the temperature sometimes reached zero. These pictures indicate just how cold and nasty it was. UPPER LEFT. On January 13 members of the 347th Regiment of the 87th Infantry Division get chow on their way to La Roche. LOWER LEFT. The barrel of this 155 mm "Long Tom" is wrapped in white cloth to match the snow. On January 14 it is being fired on German positions near Hebronval, Belgium. UPPER RIGHT. This is rough, having to hit the snow face down—but it is better than stopping the German machine gun bullets whizzing overhead. This infantry patrol of the 23rd Regiment is working its way up a narrow road near Ondenval, Belgium, January 16. LOWER RIGHT. The advancing First Army captured the important road center of St. Vith on January 23. Here, on that date, troops of the 23rd Armored Infantry Battalion, 7th Armored Division, are on the lookout for snipers in the littered streets of the town. By this time Rundstedt's salient was collapsing rapidly, though the Germans fought desperate delaying actions as they retreated back toward German soil.

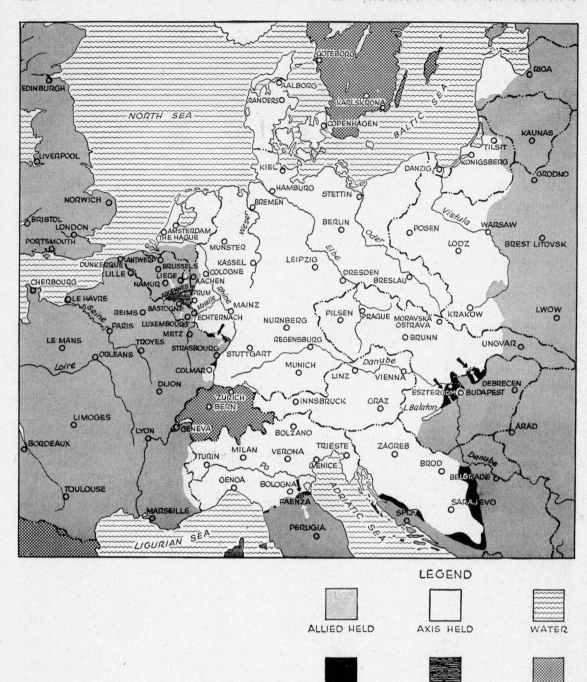

LEGEND

ALLIED HELD   AXIS HELD   WATER

RECENT   RECENT   NEUTRALS
ALLIED ADVANCES   AXIS ADVANCES

VIEWING THE DAMAGE. ABOVE. General Eisenhower and two of his most famous commanders—General Omar Bradley, left, and General George S. Patton, Jr., right—take a look at what was left of the Belgian city of Bastogne after the Ardennes offensive. The Supreme Allied Commander had words of high praise for the valiant stand the 101st Airborne Division and other Allied forces made in this besieged city during the final German offensive.

RUNDSTEDT'S FAILURE. For all practical purposes, the Battle of the Bulge was over by the end of January. The Germans had gained an initial tactical success and imposed a delay of about six weeks on the main Allied offensive. But they failed to seize their primary objectives of Liege and Namur. Their losses were staggering — 220,000 men, including 110,000 prisoners, and more than 1,400 tanks and assault guns. Allied losses were calculated at 77,000, including 48,000 wounded, 21,000 captured or missing and 8,000 killed. Tank and tank destroyer losses numbered over 700. This last bid for German supremacy stripped the Reich of all strategic reserves, and depleted German resources required to meet a powerful Soviet offensive launched in January. General Eisenhower reported that one of the most serious effects of the battle "was the widespread disillusionment ensuing from the failure to seize any really important objective and the realization that this offensive for which every effort had been brought to bear and on which such great hopes were pinned, had in no sense achieved anything decisive." UPPER. In mud and water members of the 313th Infantry Regiment, 79th Division, man a 105 mm howitzer and lob shells into German positions across the Moder River in the Hagenau area of France on February 2, 1945. LOWER. Members of the Ninth Division, occupying high ground overlooking the Urft River near Morsback, Germany, fire at Nazis attempting to retreat across the river in the face of the American advance February 4. These men are of Company L, 3rd Battalion, 39th Regiment. The big drive into Germany was starting.

FORTS AND LIBS OVER EUROPE. UPPER. Formation of B-17G Flying Fortresses (with Bendix chin-turret) of the 8th Bomber Command escorted by a P-51 Mustang long range fighter. The "L" in the triangle on the stabilizer represents the symbol for the Group, which also had a code name, such as "S" for "Silverware." The letter below the number represents the Squadron, which also had a code name. LOWER. A B-24 Liberator of the 15th Air Force drops a "stick" of 100-lb. bombs on the target of Bologna, Italy. Planes in the same flight have deposited their bombs.

TANKS AND VICTORY. The 6th Armored Division (upper) parades triumphantly through the streets of Monza, near Milan, Italy. LOWER. General Dwight D. Eisenhower, surrounded by delighted representatives of the Allied powers at Reims, France, smiles broadly after the formal surrender of the German armed forces. Surrounded on every hand by utter defeat, General Jodl and Admiral Friedeburg, representing Hitler's once-vaunted forces, signed the instrument of surrender on May 7, 1945, and brought the war to an end in Europe. The Allies then focused on Japan.

RETALIATION. The Nazi use of robot bombs forced Allied engineers to engage in the production of similar missiles. An improved version of the German V-1 is illustrated above. A United States Air Force buzz bomb, with smoke spouting from its undercarriage (upper) starts up a launching ramp, sheds its undercarriage (lower) and begins its mission.

THE FINAL BATTLE FOR GERMANY

By General Jacob L. Devers

IN February, 1945, after many months of fierce fighting, and after numerous phases of the world's greatest war were behind us, the Allied Forces in Europe stood along the west bank of the Rhine. At long last we were probing for the actual heart of the enemy. In a few short weeks we were destined to pour across the Rhine, strike out across the heart of Germany, and in conjunction with Russian forces smashing westward, to crush the last resistance from Hitler's once-vaunted armies.

Our drive to the Rhine, and the dramatic crossing at Remagen in March, climaxed more than four months of heavy fighting north of the Ardennes. From October to mid-December the First Canadian, Second British and First and Ninth U.S. Armies had fought fiercely in the Westwall defenses, the Hurtgen forest and the flooded valleys of the Roer in an effort to breach the enemy lines and drive for the Rhine.

To the south, the First U.S. Army crossed the Roer and drove across the Cologne plain toward Cologne and Bonn, while the Third U.S. Army cleared the Eifel area and occupied the north bank of the Moselle.

Before launching our armies across the Rhine for the final battles of Germany, it was necessary to clear the rich German industrial triangle between the Moselle, Saar and Rhine Rivers, the Saar and the Palatinate. Its capture was entrusted to the U.S. Seventh and French First Armies, making up the 6th Army Group under my command, attacking from the south, and the U.S. Third Army, attacking from the north. By 25 March the last German forces had withdrawn east of the Rhine; the Saar and Palatinate, and many thousands of German prisoners, were in Allied hands.

The chief crossing of the Rhine was prepared by Field Marshal Montgomery, who had been given the Ninth U.S. Army to supplement the 21st Army Group forces in his area. However, before he could finish preparations for his attack, elements of the 9th Armored Division, probing to the Rhine, found the Ludendorff Bridge at Remagen intact on 7 March. They crossed immediately to the east bank and set up a small bridgehead.

Such a windfall had been hoped for, but not at all expected. From the daring platoon leader to the Army commander who quickly redirected all his moving columns to the bridge, the prompt seizure and exploitation of the crossing demonstrated American initiative and adaptability at its best. General Eisenhower was advised of this stroke of luck, and directed that all possible forces be moved across the bridge at once. By the time of the main crossing 17 days later, the First Army held an area east of the Rhine 25 miles long and 10

miles deep, and the bridgehead became a springboard for the final offensive to come.

The Germans were now defending a line about 450 miles long, running along the Rhine from Switzerland to the North Sea. The Allied 21st Army Group faced them for about 95 miles, from Holland to Cologne; the 12th Army Group for 110 miles, from Cologne to the Neckar. The 6th Army Group front extended southward for 245 miles from the Neckar.

Meanwhile, the Third Army cleared the west bank of the Rhine from Andernach to Coblenz, and on 22 March made a surprise crossing of the river with negligible losses. The massive three-army attack in the north, preceded by a heavy air attack and the dropping of two airborne divisions, was launched successfully on 24 March.

Successful crossings were made at Xanten and Rees in the largest and most difficult amphibious operation launched by the Allies since D-Day. The Germans, diverted from the point of attack by First and Third Army crossings in the south, and hard hit from air and land, were unable to stop the crossings of British and American forces which were now prepared to sweep towards the Elbe. Seven armies almost simultaneously crossed the Rhine.

Once the Rhine had been crossed, Allied commanders turned to the general strategic plan which had been outlined in pre-D-Day planning. From the beginning General Eisenhower believed the main thrust should be made in the north with the aim of isolating the Ruhr from the rest of Germany, with a secondary thrust from the Mainz-Karlsruhe area in the general direction of Kassel. This second move was intended to hit the industrial sector around Frankfurt and capitalize on any movement of enemy units northward to meet the northern thrust. To make certain of maximum assistance, a special mission was sent to Moscow at the end of 1944 to get Russian assurance that an attack would be made on the eastern front to pin down German divisions while the drive was under way in the Rhineland. The Allied air forces gave their full backing by intensifying air attacks on German oil facilities and transportation.

The German situation, already difficult, speedily became disastrous. Allied forces, now across the Rhine in full force, quickly rushed to encircle the Ruhr industrial region. Armored elements of the Ninth and First U.S. Armies rushed eastward towards the Paderborn-Kassel area, and on 1 April linked up at Lippstadt to constitute "the largest double envelopment in history." One entire German army group and part of another, or more than

325,000 prisoners, had been seized in the pocket thus created. It was finally liquidated on 18 April.

Three routes of advance now lay open. We could push across the North German plain to the Baltic and Berlin, advance from Kassel towards Leipzig and Dresden, or go through Regensburg by the Danube Valley into Austria. We decided on a drive by the central route to cut Germany in half, isolate the country economically, and make impossible the establishment of a "national redoubt" in southern Germany.

The chief role was given General Bradley's Central Group of Armies with the Ninth, First, and Third U.S. Armies set to drive to the Elbe, seize bridgeheads over the river, and advance to the east if necessary. Operations in the north and south were limited in nature during this period. The British forces were striking for the Elbe, while my Sixth Army Group, was protecting the south flank of General Bradley's advance, and making preparations for a later advance into Austria.

By the end of the first week in April all our forces had been disposed to crush Germany, and were setting about this task. The Canadian Army was mopping up resistance in Holland; the Second British Army was driving on Bremen and Hamburg; Ninth U.S. Army was moving on Magdeburg, First Army on Leipzig, Third Army on Czechoslovakia and Austria, Seventh Army on Austria, and the French First Army on southern Germany. The newly-activated Fifteenth U.S. Army had undertaken the government of the area already conquered.

Sweeping through the area between Kassel and Leipzig over a plateau which had no major river obstacles, the Central Group of Armies by 25 April had carried out its major mission of disorganizing and defeating the German armies in its area west of the Elbe. On 11 April the Ninth Army had reached the Elbe at Magdeburg. On the 18th Third Army reconnaissance elements had reached the Czech border, and on 25 April First Army units met advance Russian elements at Torgau east of the Elbe.

To the south, the U.S. Seventh Army captured Mannheim 29 March, and advanced toward Heidelberg. The French First Army took Karlsruhe 4 April, Heilbronn and Kehl on 13 April. The Seventh Army seized Nurnberg, the Nazi shrine, on 21 April, and the French First Army occupied Stuttgart the following day. Crossing the Danube, French troops reached the Swiss border near Donaueschingen on 22 April, cutting off German garrisons in the Siegfried Line south of Breisach. On 30 April, the French First Army took Friedrichshafen and crossed the Austrian frontier at the eastern end of Lake Constance.

In the Germans' vaunted "national redoubt" area, Munich was taken by troops of the U.S. Seventh Army on 29-30 April, Passau was captured 2 May, and the Inn River crossed on 3 May, when combat patrols of the U.S. 103rd Infantry Division made contact with the Fifth Army advancing from Italy. Fighting ended on this front 5 May, with the surrender of German Army Group G.

The death of Hitler, the armistice in Italy, and the growing list of prisoners in Germany, indicated clearly that the Third Reich had crumbled, that the German Army was in its death throes, and that the long and bitter war had about run its course.

At that time General Eisenhower empowered commanders to accept the surrender of units directly opposing them on their fronts, but pointed out that any mass surrender would have to be made both to the Allies and to the Russians. Soon afterward, Marshal Montgomery and I accepted the surrender of German forces facing us, and German emissaries arrived at Supreme Headquarters at Reims to negotiate surrender on all fronts.

Admiral Doenitz, who by that time had become head of what was left of the German government, ultimately granted these emissaries power to surrender unconditionally. Surrounded on all fronts by chaos and overwhelming defeat, General Jodl and Admiral Friedeburg signed the Instrument of Surrender in the presence of representatives of the United States, Great Britain, France and Russia. At long last, and at great cost, one mission of the Allied world had now been successfully accomplished.

THE YALTA CONFERENCE. The Big Three and their staffs met at Yalta, in the Russian Crimea, from February 4 to 11, to chart the final defeat of Germany. UPPER. Prime Minister Winston Churchill, President Franklin D. Roosevelt, and Premier Joseph Stalin. LOWER. Seated at the round table are: upper left, Stalin and his aides; upper right, President Roosevelt with Admiral William D. Leahy, his personal Chief of Staff, and Gen. George C. Marshall, Chief of Staff of the Army. Prime Minister Winston Churchill, lower left, lights the ever-present cigar (note both pictures).

FUNERAL FLOWERS. This cluster of incendiaries and high explosives descends on railyards at Muenchen-Gladbach as ground forces gain in their drive towards the city. In this attack 1,250 U.S. Army Eigth Air Force B-17 Fortresses and B-24 Liberators raided 11 railyards to snarl German communications and seal off the industrial Ruhr from the remainder of Germany.

ADVANCING ON GERMANY. Try as they might, the Germans could not contain the Allied advance after the Ardennes offensive. By February 9 the Allies held a loosely defended line running along the west bank of the Rhine from Strasbourg to the Swiss border. UPPER. On February 7 infantrymen of the 417th Regiment, 76th Division, hug the walls for shelter as they advance through the streets of war-torn Echternach, Luxembourg. LOWER. Riflemen of the 4th Division ferret out Nazi snipers after having taken a small town in Germany. Rubble makes their job more dangerous.

THE RIVER ATTACK. The Germans put up a stout defense along the Roer River front, but the Ninth Army crashed through and across. UPPER. Ninth Army infantrymen hit the ground in a hurry at the sound of enemy mortar shells bursting nearby. Note the bleakness and destruction here. LOWER. Elements of the 120th Regiment, 30th Division, cross a footbridge over the Roer near Schophoven, Germany, February 23. Bridgelaying activities were hidden from view of the Germans by smokescreens thrown up by the 38th Chemical Company. Use of smoke to conceal activity is by no means new, but in World War II the Chemical Warfare Service employed advanced concepts and newly-developed devices, and its use reached points of efficiency never before attained. Smoke made decisive contributions to crossings of the Roer, Moselle, Saar, Rhine and other rivers. In each case it enabled engineers to build bridges —and the infantry to cross them— with a minimum of losses. Behind such screens, Army engineers performed miracles in providing for crossings. Yankee ingenuity often surprised the enemy. Better than that, it often completely astounded him, and afforded the Allies many advantages in their assaults.

AN ENGINEERING JOB. U.S. Army engineers claimed during the war that they could and did build anything needed. UPPER. Here, on the Roer River in Germany, is one of their jobs. This is a treadway bridge, thrown up in a hurry, but it will hold. On February 24 a tankdozer of the 750th Tank Battalion makes the first such crossing as the Allies prepared to build up men and supplies that would send them against the Germans in the final smashing blows of World War II. Note how bridge is depressed under tremendous weight of the vehicle. LOWER. Though the Ninth Army was able to surprise the Germans with their quick assault across the Roer, the going was not easy once the crossing was made. Here elements of the 29th Division crouch in the shelter of a wall to avoid heavy enemy shellfire in battle-scarred Juelich, Germany. At long last the Allied drive to the Rhine was in full swing. The U.S. First Army had captured the Erft and Schammenauel dams and swept to the Roer. Though the dams had been blown, and the river flooded, this only temporarily delayed the Ninth Army offensive, which had been launched after Allied planes had hit targets all over the entire area of Hitler's Third Reich.

ROLLING ON. In February, 1945, at the time of the Roer crossing by the Ninth Army, no less than seven Allied Armies were smashing toward the heart of Germany. In this order they were aligned from Nijmegen to Colmar: First Canadian, Second British, U.S. Ninth, First, Third and Seventh, and the French First. UPPER. German prisoners cross the Roer near Roerdorf, February, 1945. LOWER. The Riverside Cafe in Uerdingen, Germany, has really changed! Here, on March 5, elements of the 379th Regiment, 95th Division, fire from the former eatery's windows.

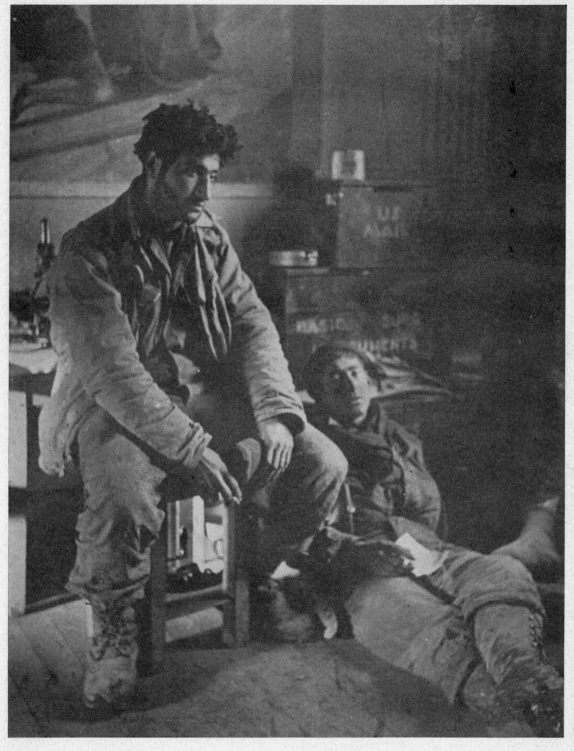

THE VICTORS. Mud caked, foot sore, battle baptized GIs
carried the war against Nazi totalitarianism from the cities,
towns, and villages of America, across the Atlantic to the
continents of Africa and Europe, and finally into Hitler's do-
main. Armed with an M-1 rifle, the infantryman walked, swam,
and crawled to meet and ultimately vanquish the enemy.

Legend
START OF OFFENSIVE
BATTLE LINE
GENERAL DIRECTION OF DRIVES
SUPER HIGHWAYS

AMERICAN 9TH AND CANADIAN 1ST JOIN FRONTS MAR. 3

AM. 9TH REACHES RHINE RIVER MAR. 2

AM. 1ST & 9TH ARMIES ATTACK AT ROER FEB. 23

AMERICAN 1ST CROSSES RHINE AT REMAGEN MARCH 7

AM. 3RD DRIVES FOR COBLENZ MAR. 3

AM. 3RD ATTACKS FROM MOSELLE LINE

ALLIED POSITION FEB. 23

AM. 7TH ATTACKS ON WIDE FRONT

BATTLE LINE

WEST BANK SECURED. By early March the great Allied offensive was relentlessly pushing the Nazis back to their last natural barrier, the Rhine River. The American Ninth and Canadian First Armies linked up in the north, Patton's Third struck from the Moselle in the south, and the U.S. First, in the center of the line, staged the most spectacular success by crossing the Rhine at Remagen, on March 7. The final days of Hitler's regime were truly drawing to a close.

ALLIED OFFENSIVE MOUNTS. As the Nazis crumbled everywhere west of the Rhine, the Allies pursued them relentlessly back across their last great natural defense line. Hitler once said, "Give me five years and you will not recognize Germany." ABOVE. These elements of the Third Army rolling through Speicher helped to confirm the Fuehrer's prophecy.

CLASH NEAR WALDAU. ABOVE. Infantrymen of the 26th Division wade through the icy waters of the Schleuse River, near Waldau, after covering their advance with machine-gun fire. The Nazi S.S. trooper sprawled in the river was caught by a burst from the machine gun. The Yanks then pushed forward to rout the enemy from dugouts in the pine forests.

THE CATHEDRAL INTACT. Through snow flurries and intermittent rains, the First Army's 3rd Armored and 104th Infantry Divisions closed in on Cologne, as the 8th Infantry Division struck for the Rhine's west bank south of the city. As American troops besieged the elaborate semi-circular defenses of the city German "Messerschmidts" hammered away at them. At 0923 on March 4, 1945, troops of General Terry Allen's Timberwolf Division became the first American troops to enter Cologne. The only familiar sight remaining in the city was the relatively undamaged Catholic Cathedral, with its towering twin Gothic spires. Large sections of the city, especially those bordering the cathedral, were utterly destroyed. Twenty-five large-scale aerial attacks had spread 42,000 tons of havoc on the city. The destruction far exceeded that wrought by the Germans on London. Two-thirds of Cologne's constructed area had been wiped out, and its beautiful streets, rent with burst sewer pipes and lined with gutted buildings, were reduced to mere paths. During the campaign which began at the Roer on February 23, and culminated with the seizure of Cologne, the 104th Division cleared 115 square miles of the German Reich, captured 97 communities, and bagged 4,899 prisoners. The joint seizure of the city by the 3rd Armored and 104th Divisions was a long awaited Allied victory and a destructive blow to German morale. With the fall of Cologne all of the west bank of the Rhine to the north, with the exception of small pockets, was brought under Allied control. To the south of the city, American units closed in on both the river and the city of Bonn, as Patton drove to within 20 miles of the Rhine and Coblenz.

THE CAPTURED CITY. The once proud beautiful city of
Cologne presented a facade of utter desolation to its cap-
tors, the First Army. The picture (above) taken from a spire
of the famous Cologne Cathedral reveals the havoc wrought
by repeated bombing attacks from the Allied Air Forces.
Cologne's Hindenburg Bridge (upper right) was destroyed
by the Nazis as they fell back across the Rhine or retreated
southward. LOWER RIGHT. Major General J. Lawton Collins
addresses men of his VII Corps in the Sports Platz at Cologne.

THE THIRD ARMY STORMS ANDERNACH. After the 11th
Armored Division of the Third Army smashed into Andernach,
Nazi snipers attempted to impede the advancing infantry.
GI's raise their rifles (upper) to silence the enemy. Two Ger-
man prisoners (lower) with their hands behind their heads
await removal to a POW camp while GIs clear the area.

BLOCK BUSTER. Neither natural barriers nor man-made obstacles deterred the Allies in their sweep to the Rhine. An American tank has just eliminated a road block. Two Nazi soldiers, for whom the war is over, lie silently beside mines they were about to plant to reinforce the obstacle. An infantryman lumbers through the gap in the road block.

THE REMAGEN BRIDGE. On the day Cologne fell, elements of the First Army's 9th Armored Division were probing to the Rhine south of the city. At Remagen these men had to rub their eyes, for they could not believe what they saw—a bridge, stout and intact! They crossed it immediately, and all moving columns were re-directed to proceed there at once. In almost a twinkling, a bridgehead was set up across the Rhine—the river that was to be so hard to cross! UPPER LEFT. On March 10 vehicles of First Army halt near Nazi sign in Remagen: "Persons who listen to the enemy and rumor mongers are traitors to the nation and as good as dead." LOWER LEFT. First Army troops and equipment pour across the Rhine on the bridge luck willed to the Allies. Two damaged jeeps are in foreground. ABOVE. The 9th Armored Division was justly proud of its exploit in capturing a bridge intact, and put up this sign so that everyone who crossed would know about it. A First Army MP stands guard beside the captured Ludendorff Bridge, the key to victory.

THE BRIDGE CAVES IN. UPPER LEFT. For several days after it fell to Allied hands the bridge at Remagen was probably the most used bridge in the world. Here on March 17 engineers put down rails. Four hours later the bridge collapsed with 400 U.S. troops on it. LOWER LEFT. A view after the collapse. Medics and engineers search for possible survivors. ABOVE. The collapse from a different angle. In addition to traffic, the bridge was weakened by German shelling. By this time the Allies held the east bank securely.

354 THE WAR IN THE ETO—GERMANY

ANOTHER OFFENSIVE. By March 11 lightning blows of the Allies had given them control of the west bank of the Rhine from Nijmegen to its junction with the Moselle at Koblenz. On March 14 General Patton established a bridgehead across the Moselle southwest of Koblenz. Next day his troops lunged southward in conjunction with a big northward thrust by the Seventh Army between Saarbrucken and the Rhine. UPPER. On March 20 Seventh Army infantrymen go across tank obstacles of Siegfried Line near Wurzbach. LOWER. Third Division soldiers advance in Zweibrucken.

CHEWING THEM UP. In spite of dense mine fields and the formidable Siegfried Line fortifications, the Seventh Army gained steadily and pinned down strong enemy formations. These, Third Army tanks cut to pieces. On March 16 a spearhead of the 4th Armored Division gained 32 miles and seized two bridges across the Nahe River south of Bad Kreuznach. UPPER. Elements of 4th Armored Division look for snipers in Worms March 20. LOWER. Members of the 275th Regiment, 70th Division of the Seventh Army, as they marched through the streets of Saarbrucken on March 21.

SECOND BRIDGEHEAD FORGED. ABOVE. In lieu of a
"Remagen" bridge, vehicles of the U.S. 87th Division, Third
Army, cross the Rhine over a pontoon bridge on March 22,
1945, thus establishing a second bridgehead on the east bank.
West of the river, the German armies had now been destroyed,
and by March 25, most of the Allied forces had pushed
across the Rhine River.

AIRBORNE CROSSING. Twenty-nine divisions, including two airborne divisions, and several brigades were under the command of General Montgomery the day he began to effect a crossing of the Rhine along the front just north of the Ruhr. On the night of March 23, 1945, infantry and tanks scurried aboard Navy LCM's and LCVP's, many of which had to be transported overland to take part in the attack. The American 30th and 79th Divisions participating in the assault front sustained a total of 31 casualties during the actual crossing. The attack by water was followed by an airborne invasion in which 1,572 troop-carrier aircraft and 1,326 gliders participated. This formidable air armada which carried the 17th U.S. and British 6th Airborne Divisions across the Rhine was protected by thousands of Allied fighter planes. At 10 A.M. on March 24, airborne troops were dropped and landed in an area 2 to 5 miles northwest of Wesel. Six bridges across the Ijssel River were captured intact, and contact was established with British units advancing eastward from the Xanten area. UPPER. Marshalling of the 17th Airborne's tow-planes and gliders at Coulmier, France. LEFT. En route to the rendezvous across the Rhine.

ADVANCE IN THE SOUTH. While the Central Group of Armies under General Bradley and the Northern Group under Marshal Montgomery were making their gains in the central and northern areas, General Jacob L. Devers, in command of the Southern Group, was crossing the Rhine in the south. The XV Corps crossed on a 15-mile front between Gernersheim and Mannheim. Elements of the First French Army crossed near Gernersheim. Both made steady gains. UPPER. Ducks ferry supplies across near Burkhein March 26. LOWER. GIs crossing Rhine near Frankenthal.

SILENT SYMPATHY. These troops of the 45th Division, U.S. Seventh Army (upper), pass in tacit commiseration as an elderly German woman stands in the street gazing forlornly at the wreckage that had once been her home. This photograph was taken in Bensheim, Germany, on March 27, 1945.

LOWER. General Patton's Third Army, smashing across the Rhine from the Oppenheim area, took the city of Frankfurt following bitter house-to-house fighting near the end of March. Here, on March 27, infantrymen of the U.S. 5th Division advance with caution during the early stages of street fighting.

NAZI DESTRUCTION. As usual, the Nazis burned or destroyed their bridges behind them at Frankfurt when the Third Army forced their retreat. UPPER. These seven bridges across the Main River at Frankfurt were blown up in the futile effort to halt the U.S. forces in late March. LOWER. Infantrymen of the 79th Division, Ninth Army, cross the damaged Einsche Canal bridge at Marxloh, Germany, March 28. The bridge had been partially destroyed by the retreating Germans; the center had been filled in by the 304th Combat Engineer corpsmen to allow passage of tanks and men. After defeating a determined enemy at Paderborn on March 30, advance elements of the First Army joined with Ninth Army troops at Lippstadt on April 1. This sealed the fate of the Ruhr, Germany's great industrial heart. General Marshall called this encirclement the "largest pocket of envelopment in the history of warfare." The skillful maneuver encircled 18 German divisions from the First Parachute, Fifth Panzer and Fifteenth Armies. In this encirclement, and elsewhere on the wide front in March, the Allies took nearly 350,000 prisoners. Germany's ability to keep up the pace of supplying the balance of her armies had just about ended.

MONSTROSITY AT MUENSTER. The marshalling yards at Muenster were a hub for rail traffic supplying the Wehrmacht opposing British ground forces in Holland and Belgium. More than 15 bombing attacks were made on them by the RAF and 8th Air Force during the war. On March 23, 1945, the day before the Rhine jump-off, 142 8th Air Force heavies dropped 441 tons square on the yards. A direct hit on this heavy locomotive left the engine jacked up in the air. By March, 1945, German carloadings had dropped to an estimated low of approximately 200,000 per week.

DEATH, DESTRUCTION AND CHAOS. For the final jump-off across the Rhine by Bradley's and Montgomery's armies the Allied air forces put on the greatest operation of the war—Rhineland Interdiction. The 8th Air Force, the RAF Bomber Command, the British 2nd TAF, and the various U.S. TACS went on the rampage during February and March, smashing everything in sight. These photos give a faint idea of how well they did what they set out to do. The railroad marshalling yards at Limburg (upper), and Siegen (lower), were relentlessly bombed into complete immobility.

THE DRIVE GOES ON. There was no halt to the Allied drive after encirclement of the rich Ruhr. The First and Ninth Armies left strong forces to contain Germans left there, then sped eastward toward the Weser River. At this stage of operations General Eisenhower told General Marshall that plans "have been developing in almost exact accordance with original conceptions." UPPER. On April 4 infantrymen and a tank of the 6th Armored Division, Third Army, advance into the town of Oberdorla, Germany, which the Division captured. LOWER. Farther to the south, a day later, these members of the Seventh Army's 42nd Division find the rubble-filled streets of Wurzburg, Germany, almost impassable. Meanwhile, the Ninth Army advance from the Weser to the Elbe was going forward at 20 to 30 miles a day against little resistance. By mid-April our troops were along the Elbe near Wittenberge and Magdeburg and had established bridgeheads across the river. Hanover and Brunswick fell to Ninth Army infantry, while the First Army, bypassing Leipzig, drove eastward to the Mulde Valley south of Dessau. The Allied avalanche grew as it rolled east and now hit the Germans from all sides.

GERMAN JACKPOT. ABOVE. One hundred tons of gold bullion in addition to millions in currency and art treasures were uncovered in a salt mine shaft situated a half mile beneath the earth's surface, near Merkers, Germany. Two German women had revealed the presence of the colossal cache to members of General Patton's Third Army. A finance officer, left, checks the money bags with a Reichsbank official.

GERMAN RESISTANCE DISINTEGRATES. After the Rhine crossing in early March, 1945, the Allied armies in the west exploited their break-through, plunging with incredible power and speed into the very core of Germany. The sweeping advance of the Allied armies is indicated by the arrows (above). The combined advances from the west and east were squeezing Germany into the shaded areas depicted on the map.

SUBTERRANEAN FACTORY. Troops of the U.S. Ninth Army
found these incomplete Heinkel jet planes in a salt mine
cavern near Engels, Germany. The assembly line, which pro-
duced between 40 and 50 of these 650-miles-per-hour planes
monthly, was situated 900 feet below the surface of the earth.
A special large elevator carried the planes to the surface.

ON THE EVE OF VICTORY. Franklin D. Roosevelt, thrice elected President of the United States, died of a cerebral hemorrhage at Warm Springs, Georgia, on April 12, 1945. The body of the Commander-in-Chief (above) was carried in state to the White House where funeral services were held, and was later interred at Hyde Park, N. Y.

FRONT FALLING IN. After the Ninth and First U.S. Armies had cleared the Ruhr pocket of more than 300,000 Germans and taken them prisoner; after one German city after the other had fallen to the invading Allies—Bremen, Hamburg, Nurnberg, Arnheim, Stuttgart; after the Third Army entered Austria, the enemy, close to capitulation, still offered resistance. Infantrymen (above) of the Seventh Army seek him in the ruins of Waldenburg, April 16, 1945.

NO HOPE LEFT. The Germans could not possibly have had any real hope of winning the war after the end of the first week in April. At that time all Allied forces had long since been disposed to crush the life out of the enemy, and were setting about the task. UPPER. The U.S. Ninth Army was driving for Magdeburg and the Elbe. Here elements of this Army's 30th Division are poised for action atop a reconnaissance car as it enters the burning town of Born, Germany, April 13. The town fell, and the Ninth rushed on. LOWER. Nurnberg, the Nazi shrine city, fell too. But it fell hard. The U.S. Seventh Army had encircled it by April 18, but its capture was delayed three days by a fanatical defense put up by German troops and civilians. When the garrison finally did give up, Nurnberg was a complete shambles. Here on April 20 infantrymen of the 3rd Division climb over rubble as they clear snipers out of the city. A tank-dozer follows them, clearing a path. The Seventh Army did not tarry long after capture of this city, but swung south into the Bavarian plain. The handwriting was on the wall—everyone knew by now that the Nazis could not possibly evade complete surrender much longer.

THOUSANDS TRAPPED. On April 1, 1945, units of the U.S. First and Ninth Armies met at Lipstadt, near Padeborn, to complete the encirclement of the Ruhr. The area's industrial capacity, by this time, had been greatly diminished, and its communications, along with the remainder of Germany, had been almost completely disrupted as the result of an interdiction program launched by the Allied Air Forces in February. The troops contained in the pocket, commanded by Field Marshal Model, made two unsuccessful attempts to forge an escape route. An American attack, launched on the 14th, bisected the pocket and on April 16, the eastern half collapsed. On April 18, the remaining troops surrendered. The number of captives taken was staggering and caused additional strain on the already overburdened Allied supply lanes. The Nazi prisoners huddled together (above) comprise a small segment of the 82,000 taken by the Eighteenth Airborne Corps near Gummersbach. At this time General Omar Bradley, Commander of the Twelfth Army Group, estimated that more than 316,000 prisoners had been captured during the elimination of the pocket. A later total revealed that 325,000 men, including 30 general officers, were taken captive. Seventeen divisions participated in this move which eliminated 21 divisions from Hitler's Army, and resulted in the capture of vast quantities of supplies and ammunition. During the latter part of April, figures disclosed that General Bradley's Twelfth Group's First, Third, Ninth, and Fifteenth Armies had taken nearly 843,000 disillusioned prisoners.

SHRINE CITY SURRENDERS. On April 16, members of the XV Corps of General Patch's Seventh Army reached the outskirts of Nurnberg. Several days of bitter fighting ensued. On the evening of April 20, as hundreds of American tanks rolled into the city, all enemy resistance ceased. The surrender of this great city, one of the oldest in Germany, constituted a great moral defeat for the Germans, inasmuch as the city had been the chief shrine of the Nazi political party. All the great party conventions were held in Nurnberg, and the enormous Nazi rallies were staged in its stadium especially erected for this purpose. The chief square of the city, the population of which numbered over 400,000 at the outbreak of the war, had been named the "Adolph Hitler Platz." Most areas of the city, including the square named after the German Fuehrer, were severely damaged. The heavy artillery shelling, necessitated by the dogged resistance of the picked S.S. defenders, contributed greatly to the devastation already wrought by Allied bombings. Nurnberg had been a key production center of the German war machine, and housed many large engineering, optical, printing, and electrical industries. By the time the Americans entered the city, most of the factories had already been destroyed by day and night aerial attacks. The picture (right) follows the progress of U.S. tanks through the rubble-strewn lanes of what had been the greatest and wealthiest city of the free imperial cities of Germany. After the conclusion of hostilities, the international spotlight was focused on Nurnberg as the site chosen for the Nazi war trials.

ADVANCE IN ITALY. By spring of 1945 Lieutenant General Mark W. Clark had been placed in command of all Allied armies in Italy. The U.S. Fifth Army was now commanded by Lieutenant General Lucian K. Truscott, and the British Eighth Army was under Lieutenant General Sir Richard L. McCreary. With strong air support the final offensive in Italy got underway April 9. ABOVE. The 370th Infantry Regiment of Fifth Army shoves off, moving through Prato, Italy. UPPER RIGHT. On their way forward, elements of the 135th Regiment, 34th Division, pass a battered church in Salvaro, Italy. LOWER RIGHT. On April 20, infantrymen move with instructions to capture a bridge at Casellechio.

THE DRIVE CONTINUES. While the British Eighth Army headed for Argenta, the U.S. Fifth, moving with speed and power, drove on Bologna. The town fell on April 21, but only after heavy and bitter fighting. UPPER LEFT. Infantrymen of the 34th Division relax in the Piazza Di La Republica, Bologna, the day the town was taken. Note the bouquets, gifts of civilians. ABOVE. On the same day elements of the 34th move out of Bologna through the Porta Saffi, in pursuit of the Germans. LOWER LEFT. The men of the 34th receive more flowers, this time as they march into Modena, on Highway 9, west of Bologna, on April 23. They had no time to rest, for the enemy was on the run.

THE TEMPO INCREASES. After Bologna, which had also been entered by Polish forces of the British Eighth Army, Fifth Army columns swept up the great highway leading to Piacenza (the ancient Via Emilia) and drove toward the Po River south of Mantua. Pursuing the enemy to the river, the Fifth Army quickly established bridgeheads on April 23. Meanwhile, the Eighth Army had met stiff resistance in Ferrara, but by the 25th they, too, had crossed the Po in force. UPPER LEFT. Members of the 85th Regiment, 10th Mountain Division, make a reconnaissance of the Po. They were planning a crossing by ducks and pontoon bridges for that night —April 23. LOWER LEFT. Sweeping on, the 10th Mountain Division entered Verona, and here on April 26 troops march down a street of the newly-liberated city. UPPER RIGHT. Another view of Verona on the same day. These Fifth Army troops are clearing the city. LOWER RIGHT. Infantrymen of the 362nd Regiment cross Adige River over an improvised bridge built beside a structure knocked out by American bombs. Groups of German soldiers refused to continue the fight and surrendered. The Allies took 40,000 prisoners at Ferrara, Modena and La Spezia.

THE MEETING AT TORGAU. Soldiers of the 69th Division (United States First Army) and members of the Russian First Ukrainian Army shake hands on a wrecked bridge at Torgau on the Elbe River. This first meeting took place on April 25, 1945. General Courtney Hodges' men had journeyed 700 miles from the Normandy beachhead while Marshal Ivan S. Koneff's men had traversed 1,400 miles from Stalingrad to cut the enemy in two in the very heart of Germany.

PUT 'ER THERE! UPPER. Lieutenant General Courtney Hodges, commanding general of the U.S. First Army, is met on the banks of the Elbe near Torgau by Major General Backenov, who commanded the 34th Corps of the Russian Army. This meeting took place April 30. LOWER. An earlier meeting—on April 26—finds Major General Emil F. Reinhardt, who commanded the 69th Infantry Division, shaking hands with a major general in command of a Russian infantry division. Note the medals the Russians are wearing and the smiles of victory that the meeting brought forth.

EAST MEETS WEST. UPPER. Second Lieutenant William D. Robertson of Los Angeles and the 69th Infantry Division of the First Army, greets Lieutenant Alexander Sylvashko of the Russian Army near Torgau on April 25. Lieutenant Robertson first saw a Red Army enlisted man on an Elbe River bridge, met Sylvashko later. LOWER. First Army Yanks and Russian soldiers walk arm in arm through Torgau after their historic meeting. This juncture of the two armies cut Hitler's Germany in two. The meeting place had been selected by both General Eisenhower and Russian officials.

DACHAU. The concentration camp at Dachau was the scene of some of the worst horrors ever visited on man. Here, for years before the U.S. Seventh Army liberated more than 32,000 who managed to survive, Nazi sadists had practiced torture and death. One of the first things U.S. troops found on the approach to Dachau—on a spur line railroad—were 39 freight cars filled with dead. Other things the Seventh Army found: A shower room where victims, thinking they were to get a bath, were gassed to death; a stack of bodies five feet high and 20 feet wide; a crematory where bodies were disposed of in production line style. Dachau was the oldest of the German concentration camps—and one of the worst. UPPER. An American flag, made by the prisoners of many countries, greeted the Seventh Army on April 30. LOWER. On the same day, an Infantry corporal of the Seventh Army distributes his last pack of cigarettes to the reaching hands of prisoners. In Dachau were French, Russians, Czechs, Poles, Germans, Italians, Yugoslavs, and others from most European countries. Their joy on being liberated knew no bounds.

DER TAG. On May 1, 1945, a German radio broadcast from
Hamburg informed the world that Adolph Hitler had given
his life in the defense of Berlin. Later evidence, uncovered
by the Allies, indicated that he had committed suicide as
the Russians were storming the city. Grand Admiral Karl
Doenitz, the fifty-year-old U-boat specialist, stepped into the
breach and proclaimed himself the new Fuehrer. ABOVE.
Hitler and Doenitz are shown as they appeared in 1942.

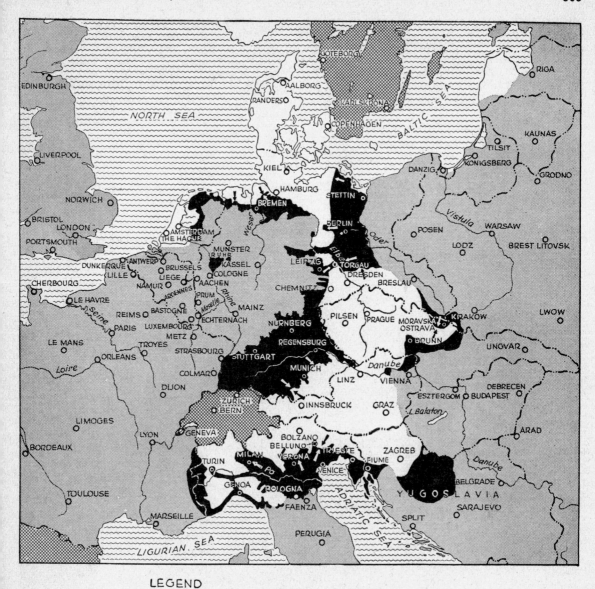

LEGEND

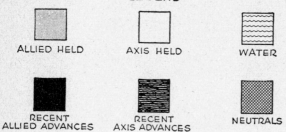

ALLIED HELD　　AXIS HELD　　WATER

RECENT
ALLIED ADVANCES　　RECENT
AXIS ADVANCES　　NEUTRALS

SOLIDARITY. As General Marshall said, the victory in Italy was a striking demonstration of the solidarity of the United Nations. At one time or another during the Italian campaign these nationalities fought under the Allied flags: Americans, British, Canadians, French, New Zealanders, South Africans, Poles, Indians, Brazilians, Italians, Greeks, Moroccans, Algerians, Arabs, Goums, Senegalese, and a brigade of Jewish soldiers. UPPER. On April 30 infantrymen of the 88th Division and tanks of the 752nd Tank Battalion pass through streets of Cornuda. A dead German lies in the foreground. LOWER. A gate separating Italy and Austria near Nauders, Austria, is scene of a meeting of Seventh and Fifth Army troops on May 7. This meeting was symbolic of the final devastation of enemy forces and the brilliant victory of the Allies. Though the whole Italian campaign had been slow and bitter, because Allied troops did not have the superiority they enjoyed elsewhere, it had finished in lightning style and had made a heavy contribution to successes on the Western front. Italy had been the scene of some of the war's hardest fighting, and the victory here was as sweet and welcome as on any front of the global conflict.

THE END AT LAST. After Marshal Montgomery and General Jacob L .Devers had accepted surrender of German forces facing them in the north and south, Admiral Doenitz sent Admiral von Friedeburg and Colonel General Alfred Jodl to Reims to surrender all forces unconditionally, as directed by General Eisenhower. There, surrounded by chaos and overwhelming defeat — the Allied armies had taken nearly 3,000,000 prisoners in March, April and May—the surrender occurred. UPPER. On May 7, Colonel General Jodl, German Chief of Staff, signs the document requiring German forces to lay down their arms in unconditional surrender. On Jodl's left in the war room of Supreme Headquarters of the Allied expeditionary Forces is Admiral von Friedeburg of the German Navy. Major General K. W. D. Strong, intelligence officer of Supreme Headquarters, stands at right. LOWER. Here is a scene from Russian headquarters in Berlin before the treaty was signed. Left to right are: Colonel General P. F. Stumpf, commander in chief of the Luftwaffe, Field Marshal Wilhelm Keitel of the German Army, and Admiral Friedeburg of the German Navy. The surrender at Reims was duplicated in Berlin on May 9.

THE JOB IS DONE. When General Eisenhower had been selected as Supreme Commander of Allied Forces at Cairo he had been directed to "enter the continent of Europe and, in conjunction with the other Allied Nations, undertake operations aimed at the heart of Germany and the destruction of her armed forces." Now his job was done, and here (upper) he makes his victory speech May 6 in Allied headquarters in Reims. On his left is the Deputy Supreme Commander, Air Chief Marshal Sir Arthur Tedder. But even with Germany defeated, there was still a big job to be done—to bring Japan to her knees, and thus end altogether the greatest war the world had ever known. From July 17 to August 2, 1945, the Big Three powers met at Potsdam to work out final plans for this job. LOWER. Here is a scene from this historic conference as it opened July 17 in a room of a modern country estate. President Truman is seated with back to the camera, with aides on either side; Marshal Josef Stalin is on the right, and Prime Minister Winston Churchill at left. These representatives composed and sent to Japan an ultimatum demanding immediate and unconditional surrender.

INDEX